Design Thinking for Every Classroom

Designed to apply across grade levels, *Design Thinking for Every Classroom* is the definitive teacher's guide to learning about and working with design thinking. Addressing the common hurdles and pain points, this guide illustrates how to bring collaborative, equitable, and empathetic practices into your teaching. Learn about the innovative processes and mindsets of design thinking, how it differs from what you already do in your classroom, and steps for integrating design thinking into your own curriculum. Featuring vignettes from design thinking classrooms alongside sample lessons, assessments and starter activities, this practical resource is essential reading as you introduce design thinking into your classroom, program, or community.

Shelley Goldman has taught elementary and middle grades, founded three schools, developed STEM curriculum and technology, and is currently Professor of the Learning Sciences and Technology Design at Stanford University, USA.

Molly B. Zielezinski works in partnership with technology companies, K-12 schools, districts, and research organizations, supporting continuous improvement by leveraging best practices from many years of research and practice in K-12.

Design Thinking for Every Classroom

A Practical Guide for Educators

Shelley Goldman and
Molly B. Zielezinski

NEW YORK AND LONDON

First published 2022
by Routledge
605 Third Avenue, New York, NY 10158

and by Routledge
2 Park Square, Milton Park, Abingdon, Oxon, OX14 4RN

Routledge is an imprint of the Taylor & Francis Group, an informa business

© 2022 Taylor & Francis

The right of Shelley Goldman and Molly B. Zielezinski to be identified as authors of this work has been asserted by them in accordance with sections 77 and 78 of the Copyright, Designs and Patents Act 1988.

All rights reserved. No part of this book may be reprinted or reproduced or utilized in any form or by any electronic, mechanical, or other means, now known or hereafter invented, including photocopying and recording, or in any information storage or retrieval system, without permission in writing from the publishers.

Trademark notice: Product or corporate names may be trademarks or registered trademarks, and are used only for identification and explanation without intent to infringe.

Library of Congress Cataloging-in-Publication Data
Names: Goldman, Shelley V., author. | Zielezinski, Molly B., author.
Title: Design thinking for every classroom : a practical guide for educators / Shelley Goldman and Molly B. Zielezinski.
Description: New York, NY : Routledge, 2022. | Includes bibliographical references.
Identifiers: LCCN 2021021632 (print) | LCCN 2021021633 (ebook) | ISBN 9780367221317 (hardback) | ISBN 9780367221331 (paperback) | ISBN 9780429273421 (ebook)
Subjects: LCSH: Problem-based learning. | Critical thinking--Study and teaching.
Classification: LCC LB1027.42 .G65 2022 (print) | LCC LB1027.42 (ebook) | DDC 370.15/2--dc23
LC record available at https://lccn.loc.gov/2021021632
LC ebook record available at https://lccn.loc.gov/2021021633

ISBN: 978-0-367-22131-7 (hbk)
ISBN: 978-0-367-22133-1 (pbk)
ISBN: 978-0-429-27342-1 (ebk)

DOI: 10.4324/9780429273421

Typeset in Optima
by KnowledgeWorks Global Ltd.

Access the Support Material: www.routledge.com/9780367221331

Contents

Acknowledgments vi
Foreword ix

Introduction 1

PART I: THE FOUR STAGES OF THE DESIGN THINKING PROCESS 17

1. **Exploring the Problem Space** 19
2. **Empathizing** 48
3. **Brainstorming** 79
4. **Prototyping Cycles** 95

PART II: BRINGING DESIGN THINKING TO LIFE IN YOUR CLASSROOM 109

5. **Design à la carte** 111
6. **Teaching Design Challenges** 120
7. **Bringing It All Together** 152

Acknowledgments

We authors met and started collaborating soon after Molly arrived from Massachusetts as a teacher at a new Stanford sponsored Bay Area charter school in 2008. We found our goals much in common, and we both had great respect for the teaching enterprise. We've been collaborating ever since, seeing many arrangements for our working relationship over the years. We are colleagues who constantly learn from each other. This book is the result of over a decade of collaboration with design thinking in K-12 classrooms around the United States and internationally.

We have deep appreciation for all of the time we spent in design thinking with our colleagues at Stanford University. Our collaborations with the d.school at Stanford helped us hone our skills as design thinkers and as design thinking educators. Susie Wise opened the doors of the d.school to us and was our first collaborator there. We went on to work with Bernie Roth, Maureen Carroll, Adam Royalty, Leticia Britos Caravango, Tanner Vea and Zaza Kabayadondo on several grants from the HPI-Stanford Design Thinking Research Program. Professors Bernie Roth and Sheri Sheppard were instrumental and inspirational partners in the work we did from 2009–2017.

Bernie, Sherri, and Shelley co-directed a grant from the National Science Foundation, dloft.STEM Learning (Science, Technology, Engineering, & Mathematics), Grant No: 1029929. Through that grant we developed design thinking for after school, camp, summer session, and teacher professional development efforts. Maureen Carroll was our project director and collaborator during those years, and we learned so much in working together. We established collaborations with teachers in the San Francisco Bay Area. We worked with Jeanne Elliot, an inspiring principal who taught us what was possible to accomplish with design thinking inside a school program. We also started working with Christelle Estrada, a specialist from the Utah State Board of Education, who collaborated with us to provide design thinking professional development experiences to hundreds of Utah public school teachers and elementary through high school students. It is our pleasure to have Christelle write the foreword to this volume.

The work in Utah was productive and generative, and much from it is reflected throughout these pages. We feel honored to have had the chance to work with all the Utah educators we met over the years. That included teachers, principals, supervisors, and people who partnered with us, especially our museum hosts and collaborators, Madlyn Larson from the Utah Museum of Natural History and Blake Wigdahl, Dave Stroud, and Lorie Millward from the Museum of Natural Curiosity.

As part of d.loft STEM Learning, we established a course in Education and Engineering, *Educating Young STEM Thinkers*. That class enabled us to have over 140 Stanford students learn design thinking and bring it to after school STEM projects with middle school students at the East Palo Alto Phoenix Academy. So much was learned through these courses, and they enabled us to develop the design thinking units and materials that are available on the d.loft website (https://dloft.stanford.edu/). Our Stanford students were amazing sources of inspiration in learning about the power of design thinking with and for middle school students. Their near peer understanding and relations with youth helped us see how habits and mindsets could be shared and learned. Special thanks go to the students that joined our team outside of class and made huge contributions to what we know and share herein: Stephanie Bacas-Daunert, Patrina Bailey, Maheetha Bharadwaj, Rasha ElSayed, Matthew Gonzales, Ben Hedrick, Michael Hornstein, Timothy Huang, Zaza Kabayadondo, David Kweck, Aaron Loh, Eng Seng Ng, Bryan Quintanilla, Saya Iwasaki, and Tanner Vea.

Megan Luce and Jason Randolf joined us in research analysis. We could not have been nearly as productive without their contributions. Some who intersected with our grants or the class went on to offer their own spins on design thinking. Rie Kijima and Mariko Yang have brought design thinking and STEAM (Science, Technology, Engineering, Arts, and Mathematics) workshops to K-12 contexts in Japan and have specialized in inspiring girls to engage in STEAM pursuits. Annie Camey Kuo, Claude Goldenberg, Rose Pozos, Melissa Messinas, and Kimiko Lange have been working in partnership with five K-8 school districts to use design thinking to innovate better instruction and services for students designated as English learners. That work has also led to many insights that appear in these pages.

Acknowledgments

Each of us authors have individual thanks as well. Shelley wants to thank Ray McDermott for inspiring confidence that all children will learn and insisting that we need to find ways to notice and support their brilliance. His confidence is infectious, and we have built a great love and life based on it. Our children and grandchildren teach us each day and keep us taking steps forward.

Molly wants to thank Zak Zielezinski for his endless leaps of faith and support as we fail forward in the endeavor designing our life together. Special thanks also to our son Kai who has taught us more about design, innovation, and inventing than either of us could have ever imagined. Finally, Molly wishes to thank each and every one of her students. It was their daily enthusiasm for design thinking and delight in the face of this new way to learn that has fueled every leg of this journey to bring design thinking to schools.

This is a long, but incomplete list. We met hundreds of teachers and students through workshops and design thinking challenges, who are not named here yet, pushed us in our thinking and understanding. We send thanks and hope that design thinking continues to influence their learning and problem-solving in the world.

Foreword

Figure 0.1 A group of students from Salt Lake City's West Side discovered design thinking. Find out what happened next.
(Credit: Christelle Estrada)

As I read *Design Thinking for Every Classroom*, it evoked so many poignant visuals, comments, and voices from Utah's nearly 10 years of design thinking for our students and teachers. I was first enamored by the design thinking mindsets and dispositions when I saw them in action. The impact on Molly's middle school students at Stanford New Schools in 2008 was unmistakably visible. I was hooked by the interdisciplinary approach when the students designed an Antarctic research station through exploring, fast prototyping, and interviewing a local Antarctic scientist from NASA. The

Foreword

students knew what they were learning, why they were learning it—an innovative design for a real-world challenge—and they knew when they were successful through the iterative process of eliciting feedback on their initial prototype.

This design thinking process to develop 21st-century skills for innovation and social entrepreneurship grabbed my imagination for possibilities in Utah's schools, especially because Utah's high school students echoed what I had heard from my own students in California: "we want to learn about the real world and be prepared for it".

Utah's design thinking professional learning opportunities began in 2010 with well-advertised studios for teams of teachers who then applied what they had actually experienced to their own classrooms. The outcome of the first experience provided a core group of first adopters with two notable participants: the Director of School Programs from the Natural History Museum of Utah, and a math teacher from a science charter school who brought a team and their principal. The Director of the museum provided the space, with a panoramic view overlooking the Salt Lake Valley, for a series of Saturday design studios and a summer design thinking academy for Utah students in grades 4–6. An avid contingent of students from a Title I school in the Rose Park community attended. With the support of teacher coaches, those students later became "experts" on design workshop teams with other teachers.

The museum summer offering was an extension of a popular after-school enrichment program. This program was an 8-week experience, meeting two times a week for 90 minutes with a skillful design thinking 6th grade teacher. We evaluated the program to understand the impact on students. The students were given surveys and participated in filmed interviews to assess the change in mindsets, skills, and dispositions. The student responses were a positive endorsement of design thinking:

> I think that it is different because you have more chances to express your thoughts, ideas, and disagreements. In school, you also don't have as much time to learn things that you might need to know if you want to get a job or to be a good interviewer. Design thinking has also changed my perspective of many things, especially the way I think of water and how much we take it for granted.–
> *Fifth Grader*

> Well there are other students in the class that I don't see a lot in the school. You think differently than [others] in your class. You get to do different stuff and

have a lot more fun than I do in class. We are in groups who really cooperate better with each other and all listen to each other talk and comment on their ideas. We try to meet people's needs in our prototypes for the clients–
Sixth Grader

It is more specific, in the way that all you do is Design Thinking. Also, everyone in Design Thinking is enthusiastic about learning, so there aren't that many distractions. That gives us more time for all the exciting activities that were planned. In Design Thinking we learned how to properly interview our client by making them comfortable and asking questions that really make them think or tell stories. We also learned how to use the information from our interview to create a prototype that fits their needs. We were taught to alter our prototypes after getting feedback from the client to make it the best it can possibly be–
Sixth Grader

The enrichment challenge found its way into the whole school. When the students interviewed teachers, parents, administrators, and the members of the School Community Council to identify the biggest challenge space for their school, they identified the school's drop-off and pick-up routines as a huge problem. As a result, the entire faculty attended a workshop to learn and implement the essentials of design thinking to solve the problem.

Shelley, Molly, and I documented a design challenge for teachers and students held at the Natural History Museum of Utah. The short documentary became a Sundance entry called: "Design Time: Learning that is Transformative". The documentary follows a group of 6th-grade students and their teachers from Rose Park Elementary School in Salt Lake City, as they design for returning veterans. This film is available in the eMedia library of the Utah Education Network (https://eq.uen.org/emedia/items/819fb03f-2639-48f6-a300-9f74dd9a14e5/1/) and on the d.loft STEM Learning website (https://dloft.stanford.edu/resources).

At the end of the film, the principal says:

I define equity as access and our students had an opportunity that they might not have had. It raised their awareness of the world around them. The biggest goal is to develop empathy and take the perspectives of others. **You launch a group of kids like that into the world and it's going to be a better place.**

To support an approach for greater dissemination in partnership with Utah's Education Network, two online design thinking courses—one elementary and one secondary—were offered to support the implementation of Utah's English Language Arts core standards. Both courses were offered over two years with cohorts of 35 educators each semester.

The key elements of the Design Thinking process became integrated in many different Utah educational settings, a university certification program for science teachers, a high school's Youth Translator program designed by the students, a business school's 1st Ascent Scholarship program, and a middle school where students in a reading class with their Design Thinking teacher/coach identified the school's challenge space as "Stress-Reduction", and at the Museum of Natural Curiosity.

Since 2010 many classrooms across K-12, including reading, math, science, and after-school programs have been engaged in design thinking. The work continues! Through the efforts of the elementary science specialist and our partnership with the Museum of Natural Curiosity, the *Doing and Talking Science* grant from the WIDA (World-Class Instructional Design and Assessment) Consortium sustains our support for Utah's multilingual learners. Five elementary school teams across Utah with well-trained teacher Design Coaches will meet in person in 2021–22. Their topic is aligned to the SEED standards in the Utah core (https://www.schools.utah.gov/file/e5d886e2-19c3-45a5-8364-5bcb48a63097) (Utah Science with Engineering Education Standards). Their design challenge is: *what does it take to survive and thrive in an environment?*

In Utah we have developed partnerships with museums and universities to create possibilities for a new vision of transformative education. This spirit of innovation with design thinking is best captured by a 6th-grade student who wrote:

> *It has changed the way I see things. I see everything as an opportunity, a chance to improve the world...Design Thinking may help you in more ways than you might think, and it can help others too. It helps you develop empathy for your client, so that you can create something that is truly helpful to them. A good prototype could lead to many things. Maybe one day, that seemingly small thing could change your life, or even the world.*

Goldman and Zielezinski provide each of us with this opportunity: to change our lives and even the world. Now it's your turn to explore, brainstorm, empathize, and prototype with your students. You will never be the same and better yet, neither will they!

Christelle Estrada

Introduction

Figure 0.2 Wooden puzzle box
(Credit: Shelley Goldman)

What Is Design Thinking and Why Teach It?

Recently, a small wooden box was received as a gift. This box is beautiful and has an intricate wooden pattern. It was beautiful but seemed ornamental because it did not open. We thought it was a showpiece we could use as a paperweight. None of us who saw the box realized that it could be opened and that it was actually a puzzle—a problem to be solved. When we were finally told, it was quite difficult to figure out, and luckily, we were given a written solution key. Once we knew that the box could be opened and it had a solution, it was an even better gift than originally thought. It could secretly hold special items. It has that wonderful feature of being an unobvious puzzle with a solution that will work to open it every time (Figure 0.2).

Finding the solutions to puzzles is a fun kind of problem-solving. Design thinking is another kind of problem-solving. Design thinking aims to solve problems that do not have working solutions or may be conducive to multiple possible solutions. These problems are different from puzzle

DOI: 10.4324/9780429273421-1

problems. They not only can have multiple solutions that can solve the problem, they also can potentially be solved in many different ways. They can be problems such as how to design a way to secretly hide precious items, and they can be problems that are huge and complex such as those aimed at mitigating climate change. In this way, design thinking is thought to be used to solve "sticky" and "wicked problems".

With design thinking you are also looking to solve problems in innovative ways—by focusing intensely on possible design solutions and by coming up with solutions that might not ever have been tried before or are unique. The wooden gift box was obviously designed as a secret box. We thought: how clever that someone made something so beautiful to help people that needed secret places to store their precious things! Designing the puzzle box was itself a design thinking solution because it meets the special needs of people in a fun and creative way.

Let's take a quick look at why design thinking problems are different from solving fixed-solution problems such as puzzles. That will help us see what is unique about design thinking and why we think it has a place in K-12 classrooms. We'll review the kinds of problems that are taken up with design thinking and how it is similar and different from other ways we approach and solve problems in the world and in the classroom. We will also introduce the processes and stages of design thinking. We will discuss the skills and mindsets we bring as designers to the problem-solving space.

What Problems Are Design Problems?

Design thinkers might try to solve problems for which there are no current solutions. The aim is to solve problems that have not already been solved or to solve existing problems in new and creative ways. We try to design new solutions that have not been tried before. Or sometimes we try to improve on current solutions.

The kinds of problems we try to solve might be local ones, such as how to improve traffic flow in front of the school, or they might be more global challenges such as how to create access to clean water in deserts or in areas suffering from drought. You might think you or your students are too young to approach such complex problems in the world, but we promise that you and they can be pleasantly surprised. We have seen kindergarteners design solutions for characters in the fairytale Cinderella, we have middle school students design an experiential museum for younger students of ancient Eygptian culture, and we have seen high school students work in partnership with a local biotech company to design patient comfort solutions. We have seen design projects focus on social studies, science, math, literature, social-emotional, and community topics. There are a range of problems that can be engaged in every classroom and at every level.

Besides coming up with solutions to problems, the actual process of engaging in design thinking helps to develop knowledge, skills, and mindsets that are important in K-12 education. Design thinkers are people who can solve complex problems. Through design thinking projects, students become introduced to and start developing and mastering a toolkit of skills, activities, and mindsets that they bring to problem-solving. They can identify problems and needs, they learn to research the problem spaces to understand current and past conditions and the ways they've been approached. They engage in empathy processes to make sure that during problem-solving, they stay focused on the needs of the people (or other beings) who will be the recipients and ultimate end-users of the design. They learn how to create prototypes for designs, how to communicate about them with others, and how to iterate and improve them based on feedback. These skills and ways to apply them are important to students.

Besides academic skills, young design thinkers also develop important working mindsets and dispositions through design thinking. They learn how to work in teams, how to think of failure as contributing valuable lessons as part of the learning process, and how to communicate with audiences outside of their classrooms. There are social, emotional, and communication-related aspects to design thinking. While many 21st-century mindsets and dispositions are important to learn and might already be part of teaching and learning in your classroom, design thinking relies on an empathy orientation. Empathy makes design thinking distinctive and it is the foundation that makes the whole problem-solving process tick. We will have much to say about empathy development throughout the book (see Chapter 2 for example) as well as other mindsets that are engaged and exercised through design thinking such as being collaborative, expecting failure to be a valid part of the learning process, having a tendency to take action, try things out, and learn to receive and pour feedback into better solutions. The mindset development clearly distinguishes design thinking from other kinds of problem-solving processes. It is one of the reasons why it is especially important for K-12 students to learn design thinking.

Introduction

We think design thinking is important training for students who will pass through their schooling years into a world that is constantly changing, not totally predictable, and will require comprehensive problem-solving at home, at work, and in the community. It helps students build their problem-solving toolkits, dispositions, and opportunities.

A Closer Look at the Components of Design Thinking

Design thinking consists of connected process steps, skills, and mindsets. It is a constellation of approaches and tools that get put to work in the face of complex problem-solving. Design thinking results in new things, new structures, new ideas, or new ways to work. It is about learning to think complexly and out of the box while also acting practically to make change through meeting the needs of people. It has similarities to engineering design and the scientific method, yet it differs from both. It is similar in being a method for problem identification and solving that involves data collection and analysis, prototyping, testing, and revision, and in being aimed at understanding and improving the world. So, what does design thinking add to your K-12 classroom?

For us, design thinking always involves an empathy-driven approach that is the key to the process. It also involves the creation of prototypes of solution ideas that get improved through the feedback of design partners. It is a process for imagining what could be, and for trying to make those visions possible. It attends to real-world situations and also aspires to result in innovations that look remarkably different than most outcomes we expect to see in classroom learning. It practices students in 21st-century competencies. Students leave design thinking challenges with a sense of efficacy because they have solved a problem for another person or group of people, and they have learned that their persistent empathy work has helped them succeed. As we see it, the look of success and pride on the students' faces is the real endorsement of design thinking. Students love that their inventions result in a contribution to another person's life and well-being. It is a process that allows students to be motivated by engagement with the needs of others, to work hard (yet in some fun ways), to think outside themselves and out of the box, and develop both social and cognitive skills along the way.

Introduction

In K-12, design thinking is closest to project-based learning, science investigations, "tech" projects, or maker experiences. It shares teamwork and collaboration. It allows students to dive deep into a topic or problem area. It enables students to have some level of choice concerning their work. Still, it is also different from each. If you have been using projects in your classroom, you and your students are already on your way to making design thinking an addition to your ways of teaching and learning. If you have not yet worked on project-based work, you can take your first steps towards that with design thinking as well.

Take a look at the Table 0.1. It compares aspects of project-based learning and design thinking. You can see some similarities and differences.

Throughout this book, we will give you practical methods to get design thinking work started in your classroom. Design thinking is actually easy to learn and practice, and that makes it achievable. You can start with small activities or projects and see your students' enthusiasm and skills building. You can do design thinking activities that will engage and inspire you and your students. Once you and your students feel inspired, you will be ready for more.

Reflection Activity

Try to see your own classroom teaching and learning experiences in the chart. You can mark the page, put sticky notes on it, or print out a copy [at www.routledge/9780367221331]. Think about these questions:

- Do you have your students collaborate in groups or teams?
- Do your students already do one or more projects a year?
- Are there opportunities for student choice?
- What in the design thinking column is of interest to you?

Highlight one or two cells (or more) where you and your students already have experience. In a new color, highlight one or two under project-based learning or design thinking that you might like to try to address. This will help you understand some of the underpinnings of design thinking and see how it is different or similar to what you have already been doing. We authors still look at this chart and find some part of our teaching story in every cell.

5

Introduction

Table 0.1 Comparison of Design Thinking, Project-Based Learning, and Traditional Learning

Component	Design Thinking	Project-based Learning	Traditional Learning
Goals	Problem-solving with possibilities for complexity, creation, and personal and social transformation	Deep dives into topics or subject, some development of "expertise"	Learning and accountability of prescribed and pre-chosen knowledge
Method	Multiple-step, iterative process that emphasizes research on relevant topics, empathy and hands-on prototyping, and feedback for generating solutions	Questions, problems, or concentrated inquiry, involve student personalization or choice	Introduction of content or concepts to be learned. Transmission from teacher to student
Pedagogy with roots in…	Real-world problems and design partner's considerations, theories of learning that rely on social activities	Investigations, making, and knowledge creation, constructivist meaning making on the part of students	Didactic teaching, idea that certain knowledge exists and can be taught
Creation Process	Collaboration-based, hands-on, prototype central, relies on mindset development along with content exploration	Ideas of deep dives into knowledge and investigations, some personalization and student choice that may be individual or collaborative	Received knowledge and application through testing of individual performance of indicators of learning
Innovative problem-solving and 21st-century mindset development	High and regularly occurring through reaching beyond what already exists	Expectation of some sophistication and complexity in student process and product	Limits exist based on predetermined content and complexity determined by teachers

Introduction

 ## A Look Closer Look at Design Thinking

Table 0.1 showed you that design thinking has certain characteristics. You can see that design thinking is applicable when there could be multiple solutions to a problem. Sometimes the problems are very complex and may not have current solutions. The problem process involves learning and developing skills, processes, and mindsets. The key that makes the whole process tick is empathy development. Design thinking problems involve making choices and learning to collaborate.

A Closer Look at Design Thinking Problems

Design thinking problems are based in human and ecological needs and always involve an empathy process. They have multiple and varied solutions. They may be aimed at:

- Designing and developing technologies or products
- Conceiving of systems or communication structures
- Designing and creating physical structures (from space in the classroom, school, playground, garden, community)
- Applying disciplinary knowledge to design (e.g., maths for architecture, science to medical protocols, engineering to emergency shelters, history to new policy)
- Making and creating artistic projects (e.g., creating art, music, dance, performance, fashion)
- Writing and interpretive projects (e.g., character studies, alternative stories, fan-fiction, fiction)

On the other hand, it is sometimes useful to understand the kinds of problem-solving that are *NOT* design thinking challenges, such as:

- Solving puzzles/problems that already have structured solutions (volcano demo and other demonstrations of science concepts, running experiments where outcomes are already known)
- Using algorithms to solve given math problems as opposed to using math as part of solving a real applied problem

Introduction

- Completing basic research and analysis (in science, history, etc.)
- Closed end engineering problems (single answer problems or those with specified designs)

Stages of the Design Thinking Process

In understanding design thinking, it is helpful to start with the methods. We use the metaphor of a stage and stages for understanding the design thinking process. We think about a stage as a place or time in the design process. It is also a place from which you are set to engage in particular aspects of the process. Each stage gets set for the kinds of scenes and action it supports. We introduce the mindsets separately in order to make design thinking teachable. To us, it is like breaking a complex problem into its constituent parts before asking students to act on the complex whole.

Ultimately, learning the components of the design thinking model in isolation is not sufficient, so later in the book we will take you through design projects in full to help you get the idea of how the stages and components can be applied in concert and as they are needed to move the process along. There are parts of the design thinking process that are central. We call each of them a stage. Each stage has a profile. It has a few aims, some attached methods and skills to learn and apply, and some mindsets and ecological concerns that should be considered part of the performance of the stage (Figure 0.3).

When you are employing design thinking, you will be moving from stage to stage, pulling in and integrating mindset and content development, and keeping in mind contextual and equity concerns. We will teach you how to manage some of these demands and take them up with your

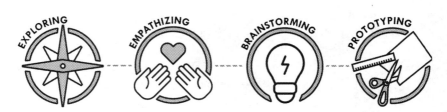

Figure 0.3 Stages of the design thinking model
(Credit: Saya Iwasaki)

students. We will start with a tour through the stages and we will take them in a possible order, but ultimately, we do not want you to think of the stages as static or as falling in a specific order.

The aim is for you to move beyond simply teaching stages in the process in a linear fashion to providing students with experiences that include empathy development, participation in team collaboration, and content learning from each stage of the problem-solving process. We hope that design thinking helps your students develop a sense of efficacy, and the persistence to try again by stepping onto the different stages as they need them to make progress and meet their design goals.

Performing work on each design thinking stage will help your students experience dispositions and ways of acting that they can carry with them through the rest of their education and beyond. These more integrated aims involve skill development that is synergistic with mindset development—the epistemological viewpoints that represent changes in learners' orientations as thinkers and actors. One does not become a design thinker simply by implementing the stages in the method. There are also moments of significant insight that shift learners' thoughts and actions during problem-solving. In this way, design thinking is complex. It involves learning the method—skills, concepts, and stages—and developing dispositions for thought and action. The process involves learners empathizing with specially selected design partners, learning to work collaboratively, and employing their hands, minds, and intuitions in ways that drive creative problem-solving.

Design Thinking Process, Skills, and Mindsets

Design thinking comprises a set of processes, skills, and mindsets. The process can be described in many ways. We like the idea of viewing it as a series of stages. We emphasise the processes, the mindsets, and the other contextual factors you will be considering with your students while engaging each stage.

There are debates about which elements of design thinking should be taught and are essential to the practice. The model we teach in this book is adapted from the version taught at The Hasso Plattner Institute of Design at Stanford University, also known as the d.school (see d.school.stanford.

edu). Our framing is based in the d.school representation of the process because we have partnered with the d.school and they have spent over a decade working with K-12 teachers on their model. Our model differs slightly but remains attached in spirit. Let's examine the elements.

Stages in the Design Thinking Process

Exploring the Problem Space

A problem space is the broader area of focus in a design challenge. They can be rooted in many contexts and in almost any content area of the curriculum. We have worked with problem spaces as broad as these topics: access to clean water, designing shelters and structures (pet shelters, Antarctic research stations), problem-solving for character from literature, inventing mobile and wearable technologies, and rethinking school cafeterias. Exploring problem spaces helps to spark the students' interest and immerse them in the design challenge. In each case, the aim is to make the students aware of and develop knowledge of the larger problem space associated with the design and some of the current ways solutions are being applied. Learning about the bigger context of any design problem may be one of the initial stages to visit when starting a challenge. It may also be one that you return to and develop throughout.

Working on the background stage gives us opportunities to understand the pre-existing knowledge that students are bringing to the new challenge and what might be appropriate for them to learn next. Taking the time to build on prior knowledge or establish a baseline of working knowledge helps us and the students to set the stage for deeper understanding, complex thinking, and problem-solving. Background research helps students give them the opportunity to establish some basics. It also provides them with research and communication skills.

Empathizing

Design thinking is distinguished from other classroom learning experiences by its reliance on empathy development and insights for motivating the process. Empathy is the experience of understanding another's conditions by identifying with that person's experiences and perspectives. It is a factor in prosocial stances, to helping others, and to responding and acting compassionately. It is most useful to design thinking. Ultimately, it ensures that produced designs will actually work for people and will meet their needs. This is important, and the idea of user-centered design is now a standard across most professional design ventures. We also think that it is essential in K-12 schools because empathy helps teach our children how they can make contributions to others and the collective well-being. It gets them to think about others and their needs. It teaches them that they can operate in the world outside of self-centered concerns and modes of action and into reciprocal relationships and relevant accountability with others. It leads to both better designs and better students!

Design thinkers develop empathy by observing and interviewing potential end-users of their solutions, watching and listening carefully, collecting artifacts, and learning through exercises how to make inferences and derive insights about people's needs and experiences. It is often said that the late Steve Jobs, co-founder and CEO of Apple Computer Inc., could figure out what people needed or wanted before they could articulate it themselves. It's like saying that sometimes people cannot see the forest for the trees. People are too close to their lives to always see their own big picture. We like the formulation of the empathy process helping designers understand the people for whom they are designing—achieving those insights that can even surprise the people they are about in confirming ways. That is the level of empathy and insight for which design thinkers strive. There are processes and tools to help learners develop inferences, and even young designers can be successful. Empathy can create connections between the designer and the people who they partner with as design end-users.

Once designers mine their empathy insights about those they are designing for—who we call their design partners—they use the insights to create a statement that defines those needs in a specified solution space. An example of a Point of View (PoV) statement from a team is "Dedicated, kind, and never tiring, Colonel B needs a way to help veterans of war adjust to their communities when they return from battlefield deployment". The statement, written by upper elementary students with teacher support, becomes an essential tool for explicitly defining the problem that the design team then works to solve. It is an explicit statement about what has been learned about the design partner, their needs, and a possible solution space that can be focused on, yet still be open to multiple possible solutions.

Introduction

Brainstorming

To brainstorm—to generate ideas, to imagine, or to conceive—is a set of processes for generating and evaluating many ideas that could be solutions to the focused defining statement for the design challenge. The process is dominated by the brainstorming of possible solutions. This is a fun and generative process that you and your students will enjoy. We teach design thinkers to always generate many ideas in this stage. We always say that, in brainstorming, "no idea is a bad idea". We teach designers to generate many ideas, even those that might seem impractical or far-fetched. The brainstorming stage is full of fun and creativity. We teach that there are rules to brainstorming and there are goals. The rules guide the members of the design team so the process can move forward productively and the goals are set high to force the designers to push and reach further. Rules might include simple guidelines such as: no judgments during brainstorming, wild and high-risk ideas are welcome, and find ways to build on and expand on the ideas of others. The goal of brainstorming is to be extremely generative and push for range and quantity first, then to understand the possibilities before setting solution directions. The final goal is to make sense of the brainstorming possibilities and help students identify their favorite ideas, consolidate similar ideas, and prioritize the design solutions they would like to develop further.

Prototyping & Testing Cycles

Prototypes are representations of solutions that help our young designers communicate their design ideas to their design partners and other possible end-users. They make solution ideas tangible. There are many kinds of prototypes—models, storyboards, experiences, or physical spaces to name a few. In school-based design thinking, we usually engage in creating and then communicating with low-resolution prototyping. Low-resolution prototypes are mock-ups or first drafts that are usually hobbled together with locally available materials. While used professionally, low-resolution prototypes are the perfect materials for K-12 students to use for representing and communicating about their design ideas. The aim is to convey the solution idea and to gather feedback that will be poured into a next iteration of the solution. While our experience is that students have wonderful ideas that delight or even deeply touch their design partners, there is always an expectation that the success of a prototype will always be partial. The communication with the design partners over the prototype sets the stage for revisions and iterations.

Testing is the process of sharing a prototype with the design partner or others and receiving feedback. This is an essential part of the prototyping stage. The solution idea may need small improvements or added features, but generally, prototypes need improvements or even rethinking. This is never considered a "failure". In design thinking, students learn that failure and iteration with visits to and from different stages of their work are a major part of the learning and design process.

In design thinking, the students learn that being willing to make adjustments and pivot is key to the process and to finally meeting their design partners' needs. The stages and their constituent activities sometimes have them extremely focused and sometimes have them thinking more expansively. They are very focused when they are on the empathy stage, and they are thinking expansively when they are on the brainstorming stage. While on every stage, they learn how to use tools they are acquiring to exercise them, keep them on task, think openly, and develop knowledge and insights about both the problem space they are working in and about their design partner's needs.

Mindsets

Mindsets are the skills, dispositions, and ways of thinking and acting on problems that the design thinker develops and applies in problem-solving. They can be thought of as comprising the meta-cognitive or "thinking" part of design. While there are many helpful mindsets, three that are important for young learners involve: (1) learning to fail forward, (2) work collaboratively, and (3) develop a sense that one can make change in the world.

Learning to fail forward is extremely important in solving complex design problems. The testing phase ensures that the design results in iteration or new ideas that are even more responsive to the design partner. In schools, students learn that failure is to be avoided and that success is rewarded. Our emphasis in schools is often on "getting the right answer". Design thinkers believe that failure is an essential part of learning and that attuning to various failures informs better design.

Introduction

Learning to work on a team is essential to 21st-century competencies. Design thinkers are encouraged to engage in "radical collaborations"—those that bring together people with diverse views and skills. Team diversity makes an impact during every aspect of the design thinking process, from working with the design partner to brainstorming multiple solutions to prototyping and iterating solutions.

Besides learning a process and skills for solving complex problems, developing creative confidence is an aim. Students who have developed creative confidence act on the world as young children do, with a sense of wonder and exploration, and divergence of stimuli, and through experimentation and even risk. Design thinkers attempt to keep these innovation-relevant mindsets evolving in children of all ages. Creative confidence can be relearned through the design-thinking process.

What's in this Book?

In the remainder of the book, we will give you more detail on each aspect of the process and help you start putting together activities and design thinking projects you can use with your students. Each chapter will introduce you to a stage or aspect of design thinking. It will explain each, tell you about why we think it is important, and help you find ways to put it into practice with your students. You will read stories from our own work with design thinking and see examples of activities and materials you can use. There will be links to the materials so you can download them online and put them to use.

The next section of the book takes us through the stages of the design thinking process. Chapter 1 is about exploring the problem space that you will address through your design thinking work. It takes up two main topics. The first is how to define and understand your problem space when you prepare to start a challenge. It explains why it is so important for you and your students to become well-versed in the problem spaces where you will be working. It shows you the ways you can make the exploration of background knowledge an important and worthwhile goal. This is an essential design practice, but also such an important connection to content learning for your students that is relevant to the design challenge they will be taking up. We will show you how the design thinking process integrates with the content, communication, and research skills your students need to be building. We provide some nuts and bolts for how to think about and manage your class as a design space, how to establish student design teams, and how to set up a design journal process for the students.

In Chapter 2 we discuss empathy and its centrality to the design thinking process. We explain what empathy is and why empathy is so important to the design thinking process and why it is so important for your students. Empathy is discussed as both a stage in the design thinking process and a mindset to be learned, making it a key aspect of the whole design thinking enterprise. We make a case for why empathy is an important building block, and we share stories of how it has driven students to become motivated in design challenges and also to work with focused insight. We will help you practice your own empathy muscles and give you exercises and activities you can put to use with your students. It is important that students not only gain empathy, but can be guided in activities that will help them evolve their empathy insights into focus for their design solutions.

In Chapter 3 we move to the brainstorming stage. Brainstorming is the generation of many ideas that could be possible solutions. Brainstorming is fun and generative. Even so, there are rules that we will go over that will keep brainstorms productive and on track. We will discuss several ways you and your students can brainstorm, and we will illustrate successful brainstorms that we have found to be inspiring.

In Chapter 4 we take you through prototyping and feedback cycles. We explain the purpose of prototypes and how they can function. We also give you guidance on ways that you and your students can collect and manage feedback and turn it into revisions, iterations, or new ideas that they can move forward.

Part II of the book is dedicated to building your confidence and helping you get started with design thinking. These chapters are filled with examples of design thinking activities and advice for bringing them into your lessons. They will help you introduce everything from one-time design-relevant activities to full curriculum units that can take weeks to complete with your students. Chapter 5 is full of those activities that you can use immediately to start building design thinking skills and mindsets. The chapter will help gather and organize the materials you will need to organize and have available to your students. It will also help you make the linkages between your design thinking activities and the standards.

Chapter 6 details three levels of design thinking challenges. Although we take a multi-graded approach in general, we break out activities in the

Introduction

chapter that are well-suited for younger (K-5) and older (6–12) students. We have activities for one-hour challenges that we call Shorts, day-long challenges that we call Features, and deep-dive unit level challenges that we call Series. They range in topics and we share the ways you can adapt them to your grade level and subject concerns. Once you try these activities and others profiled throughout the book, you will be becoming a teacher who is comfortable with and seeing the benefits of design thinking.

We think you are ready to learn more deeply. Enjoy!

PART

The Four Stages of the Design Thinking Process

1 | Exploring the Problem Space

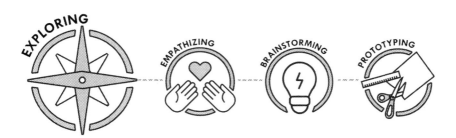

Figure 1.1
(Credit: Saya Iwasaki)

In 2013, Shelley and I stood before a group of 40 students, teachers, parents, and school leaders just outside of Salt Lake City, Utah. We were leading a design thinking professional development (PD) to support this diverse group of stakeholders in jump starting the process of bringing design thinking to life at their school. Other than the principal, who had invited us, this group had no background in design thinking.

We created mixed design teams of five individuals, making sure each team included at least one teacher, student, parent, and school leader. This workshop would engage our learners through participation in a start-to-finish design challenge with their teams.

We started with some team building activities and then hit the ground running by introducing the **problem space**. A problem space is the broad area of focus in a design challenge. In this workshop, the problem space was *shelter*. We advanced rapidly through a slide deck that walked teams

Four Stages of Design Thinking Process

through definitions, purposes, and unique examples of shelters (see Figure 1.2 for excerpt from Shelter Slide Deck). We presented the teams with shelter-related questions that were meant to spark their interest. For example, we showed them pictures of igloos, caves, and houseboats. Then we engaged the team members in a think-pair-share activity in order to place some examples of shelters on a 2 × 2 matrix, deciding the extent to which shelters were either temporary or permanent and necessary or desired (see Figure 1.3 for visualization of this 2 × 2 matrix).

We immersed the teams in the problem space before we posed the specific details about the upcoming design challenge. The idea was to hook them with varied visual examples, engaged discussion, and by tapping into their prior knowledge. This initial process was the first step in building background. Building background is the first phase of the design thinking process in K-12 classrooms. In the rest of this chapter, you will learn more about why it is important to build background, how to do this work as a teacher, and specifically how the standards for learning can be inspirational and utilized as you engage in design thinking with your students.

What Is Background Building?

We always start classroom design thinking challenges with background building. We believe it is essential for K-12 learners. We both are "learning researchers", and the work in the field tells us that preexisting knowledge is variably present and can be fashioned quite successfully into new learnings. Students come into the classroom with preexisting knowledge, experiences, skills, and beliefs about the world and how it works. They may have particular ways in which they interpret information or events depending on their prior knowledge. When we take time to build on prior knowledge or establish a baseline of working knowledge, we will be doing the students a service by helping to set the stage for deeper understanding, complex thinking, or even innovative problem-solving. When we begin a design thinking challenge, we cannot assume that students have the necessary background knowledge on a problem space topic, so it's best if we give them the opportunity to establish some basics. In design thinking, we often talk about working in collaborative groups where students can bring various skills and prior experiences. We are also keenly aware that in classrooms, we need to open opportunities for all the students to achieve

Exploring the Problem Space

Figure 1.2 Background building excerpt from Shelter Challenge Slide Deck
(By: Molly B. Zielezinski)

Four Stages of Design Thinking Process

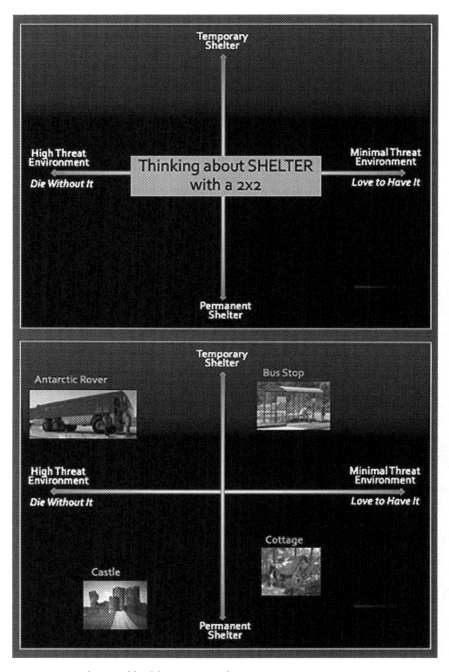

Figure 1.3 Background building exercise featuring 2 × 2 matrix
(Credit: Molly B. Zielezinski)

goals and meet and go beyond standards. In our shelter design thinking challenge, we built background knowledge for the students even though we knew they were working with teachers in small groups. This was meant for all—the students got to define what shelters were and understand some of their requirements and features, and the teachers on the teams had their knowledge refreshed and were able to be reminded that there are as many types of shelters as there are people and situations.

Establishing background knowledge in the design thinking problem space particular to the challenge also provides students with opportunities to experience research and develop important research and communication skills. If background research is done as an expectation at the start of design thinking challenges, students will surely develop the skills to delve in and find new and interesting ways to do the research and share their results. As you will see later in this chapter, there are unlimited ways to build background knowledge with students, depending on their age and skills. In the early grades it might mean looking through picture books or hearing a story being read; in the later grades it might involve independent research with reports to the larger classroom or interviews with experts in the field.

Building background knowledge can also be an opportunity to make connections among the subjects and content areas. It is a perfect opportunity for reading and literacy work in the content areas. We have built background by bringing the students in contact with literature, social studies, science, and math. In the shelter focused challenges, we have integrated engineering information about the features of shelters, such as which shapes are efficient in certain circumstances, and why triangles are important for strength. We've done experiments about climate and insulation, and read about shelters in different cultures and for different populations.

Like other stepping stones in the design thinking process, research and activities for background building can take place at the beginning of a challenge and also be woven through the projects. One of our favorite models is to start off, then intersperse background building activities as the challenge is developing.

In a design thinking project, it is necessary to build background so that designers can learn about the places where the design space is already saturated and places where there are unsolved issues, problems, or opportunities. Because design thinking strives to bring innovative, new solutions into the world, becoming informed about what already exists is helpful. It makes much more sense to innovate once you know where the thinking or concepts involved in any problem space currently stand. This is true whether you are a newbie or an experienced design thinker.

How to Build Background

As we have discussed, the first stage of the design thinking process is building background. Having all the students building background on the topics related to the challenge is an essential goal. As your students encounter problems in the classroom and problems in the world, they will be tempted to jump right into solutions. We find that adults are like this too. It seems like we are hardwired to confront new problems head on. Sometimes we do jump in and act on the spot, and that can be a healthy and invigorating response. Other times, we need to take time to understand the complexity or history involved in a problem that we are trying to solve. We also want to see the problem space from many angles and vantage points. That is not to say that we should not act in energetic ways in the problem-solving process. In design thinking, we sometimes call on instinctual or quick responses to understand this such as when we are creating energy through improv or creating solutions through brainstorming. Yet in this stage, we begin to develop deep and varied understandings of a topic. In design thinking, we try to gather background context before we begin to resolve problems and continue learning throughout the process. Before digging into solutions, experienced designers linger in the ambiguity of the context.

Here is an example of building background from Molly's classroom when she worked with middle school students in an underserved California community. Molly was working on her very first design challenge (that had been developed by a team Shelley worked with through an NSF middle school math curriculum project and then revised by the REDlab team). The problem space in this challenge was to design a shelter in Antarctica for scientists to do their work **over** winter. We know that there is a lot of information about the conditions in Antarctica and several shelters for scientists, such as the McMurdo Station that has been operating since 1955. Still, the Antarctic environment is always changing and new kinds of science being done are also placing demands on the shelter design and its impacts on the environment.

Exploring the Problem Space

For middle school students, building background means setting the stage and becoming acquainted with the problem space. In the case of Antarctica, it means to do it as an explorer who is charting a new territory. Antarctica turns out to be a wonderfully rich topic for middle school students. It is a distant, yet compelling environment. So, when we began the Antarctica project, Molly started by asking her students what they already knew about Antarctica. They charted basic information that they could contribute—cold, snow, penguins, continent, bottom of the earth etc. Most of the students participating were born in warm weather climates and had very little real-life experience relevant to these topics. Of the 60 students across 3 classes, fewer than 10 had first-hand experience with snow.

To build from this baseline, Molly showed the students videos of the conditions of Antarctica and brought in an Antarctic scientist who worked at a NASA research center nearby to speak with them. He offered first-hand accounts of his expeditions, let the students try on his gigantic weatherproof boots, and answered a never-ending stream of middle schooler questions. Molly also created presentations to increase student awareness of the essential contextual factors at play in Antarctica. At the time, Molly was new to design thinking but learning through experimenting with various classroom challenges. This process was enriched by library books, maps, primary sources from digital archives, hand-picked collections of digital resources, and student-curated digital content collections. Molly decided that she would try to find ways to connect students online with other scientists and experts who were willing to outreach to students.

At the end of the background building introduction, Molly's stage was created in the classroom. It had an Antarctica corner displaying the newly expanded knowledge of the context for which students were designing. Students continued to build on this corner throughout the Antarctica challenge, and it served as a visual representation and depository of the class' collective insights about this problem space.

Setting the Classroom Design Set

The Antarctica stage turned out to be an important space for the students during the challenge. The students visited, looked at the materials, and used them to justify or confirm their emerging ideas. Knowledge building spaces are already well known and desired in classrooms, especially when there is a major unit or topic to be studied or project work is about to take place. If you have a school library, the materials there and the librarians can be quite helpful. If your students are mature enough and have web access, the class can be building background and improving their search skills while developing some online space for background materials.

While the background building corner was important, it was one of several staging arrangements needed for accomplishing the design thinking challenge. Whether your design thinking topic is Antarctica, shelter, access to energy, community gatherings, or even improved lunches in the school cafeteria, the design thinking classroom demands some hybrid stage sets.

What Other Classroom Stage Sets Are Needed?

Design thinking will have you staging your classroom in creative ways. Each stage of design thinking has accompanying activities that will have space requirements.

Staging the Room for Collaboration

Design thinking activities are collaborative in nature. Students will work in teams, so group working spaces are important. You will need spaces for groups to sit and spaces for them to stand. Wall spaces that can be made into "writeable" spaces used by groups during activities are especially helpful. If you have white boards, that is an obvious place to establish some working space for teams. Some classrooms secure poster paper to walls for groups, and we have sometimes used silicon plastic that clings through static and is writable with dry erase markers to create writable wall space. You can also use small sticky notes to write and then post them on white boards, walls, doors, or windows. These are the spaces and places where groups will be recording ideas and thinking out loud. They also can stay in place, so all students in the class can see the in-process outputs of their activities. These crowded and busy wall spaces will bring the design thinking process to life. They will make work and thinking visible, they will "convince" you and your students of the work going into their eventual solutions, and they will provide opportunities for documentation of their processes. Your students will feel like they are living in real creative, design spaces (as they should). Some classrooms have open wall space, some do

Exploring the Problem Space

not, but do not worry. There are ways to create wall-like spaces for groups and their collaborative work in any room. Doors can be used. Turning tables upright on their sides can provide a writeable space. Hallways or exterior walls are options in some schools. If your classroom cannot be used, you might take your class to the multi-purpose room, cafeteria, or auditorium for some collaborative sessions.

Our one bit of advice is to make sure you have some spaces where groups can stand and do collaborative work. We fully expect that some collaborative work will be done at tables of desks that are arranged for small groups. We implore you to make the students stand when they are doing the generative team activities, such as brainstorming, that are necessary in design thinking. Research does show that people are more creative when they are standing or walking, and we definitely observe higher energy when we have students up and out of their seats for empathy, brainstorming, and prototyping work. So, try to remember to make the effort to establish writable vertical surfaces for some of the collaborative work. They will get the most from it if you do.

The student teams will need spaces for brainstorming and building prototypes, and staging those activities demands different kinds of spaces.

- **Empathy-related staging:** this includes interview space, observation, empathy interrogation work (charting, full-body empathy charts—floor and wall space)
- **Prototyping materials space:** includes space and organizational structure to store building materials and prototypes in progress
- **Space to build prototypes:** this includes robust physical space for teams to collaborate on building and practicing. It must accommodate performance, paper, models, and life-sized experiences
- **Venues for feedback sessions:** these include space for each team to sit down with a user, present prototypes, and gather feedback on their work in progress.

For each type of stage, keep in mind that floor space and wall space is always helpful and can be arranged in new ways to support the design thinking project. Students should be able to access sources and resources that are needed as part of the project (see next section). Additionally, students should be able to access a physical space where they are keeping a record of their team's progress on the design challenge. Digital spaces such as google drive folders or collaboration software can serve as supplements to physical team spaces but design thinking projects thrive when given at least some physical space to catalogue the process and progress of a team.

Sources and Resources

When you approach a new design challenge, in the classroom or in life, you begin by casting a wide net. The collective human experience has likely mired around in this problem space before, and our local community and the wide-open internet gives us access to a deluge of relevant information. The teacher's role in building background is to be the director of knowledge. This is like being an air traffic controller, but instead of organizing information about flight paths and runways, you are organizing information about your problem space. As director of knowledge, you sift through a lot of resources and direct those that are relevant back toward your students.

This does not have to be an overwhelming task. You do not need to read the whole internet to be a good director of knowledge. In fact, there are many reliable and relevant sources you can turn to when beginning this process. You can use this list to create a well-balanced menu of digital and real-world resources, experiences, and human connections while you plan phase 1 of your design challenge. And don't forget the students themselves. Depending on their age and skills, you can let them find, gather, and report on resources about the challenge. The research experience can reinforce their skill building.

Digital Resources

- University library websites, specific content collections
- YouTube, TeacherTube, and Vimeo
- Non-profit websites
- Public television websites
- NASA educational resources
- NOAH real-time data
- National Archives online

- Topic-specific social media groups
- Apps
- Teacher groups on social media (active communities on Twitter, Facebook, and Instagram)

Physical Resources

- Local libraries
- Local museums
- District and county offices
- School curriculum leaders
- Local community college departments
- Local experts
- People in your network (friends of friends, family, colleagues, etc.)

If you know that your best friend's great-uncle Marvin is a retired chef and you are about to start a project related to food and culture, ask for an introduction. The worst that can happen is for someone to say no. This is true for all the physical resources, not just network connections. If you are starting a new project, do not hesitate to fire off a dozen emails explaining your mission and asking for resources, Zoom calls, or further suggestions. Librarians love helping and are generally honored to be asked. District and county education offices often have curriculum collections and other untapped resources lying around. You can even find a relevant expert on LinkedIn and message them about a genuine opportunity to transform the lives of the next generation if only they would just attend a 30-minute Zoom Q and A with the class. People who don't spend every waking moment with school-aged children are typically open to doing a small part for the good of the world's youth.

Recently, I was advising a team of 2nd grade teachers who were designing a challenge about the river running behind their school. One teacher described a bit of local folklore to me and said she heard this was documented somewhere within the local historical record. She said she had dreamed for years of getting her hands on this document. After 5 minutes of Googling, I found the document at a local university library. The teacher emailed the librarian and 15 minutes later, she has a PDF copy of the primary source written in the 1800s. The point of this story is that resources are abundant and once you get clear about what falls within the wide net of a problem space, there is no limit on what you can gather to build relevant context for your students.

Setting Up Student Design Teams

Setting up the student design teams for a challenge can be as important as setting the stage with background materials and setting up the physical space. It is worthy of thought and management.

One hallmark of design thinking is that it is a collaborative endeavor. Design thinkers like to talk about the successful process relying on and requiring "radical collaboration". What is radical collaboration, and why is it so important to design thinking? Radical collaboration is the process of bringing together people with diverse skills, backgrounds, and perspectives, so that the different points of view can be marshaled to provide many alternatives for moving the design process forward and toward innovation. The design thinking process relies on letting the differences among the team flourish while also being harnessed for the benefit of the designs. The thinking is comparable to the rationales for heterogeneous groups in the classroom where the diversity is considered to be stimulating and shows positive results for all members no matter what skills they have when they enter the group.

There are as many ways to think about groups in the classroom as there are solutions in a design thinking problem. Sometimes forming groups can be a sticky problem. You might see good results, but there are also times when groups are not successful. Our goal is to help you think about how you want to form groups for design thinking activities in your classroom. Rather than give you hard and fast rules, we will provide you with a few ideas about teams and a bit of advice about putting them together. Let's start with a few things we know about group work from research.

One of the most important general findings from educational research on teams, collaborative learning, and cooperative group work is that they support more academic learning and achievement across the subject areas for their student participants. Reviews of research over many years have concluded that collaborative learning studies have demonstrated results such as higher critical and creative thinking, confidence, social acceptance of those who are different, interpersonal skills, and intergroup relations (two reviews of interest include Davidson (forthcoming) and Cohen (1994) for a concentration on equity issues in group work). With the research documenting the general efficacy of group work, you can feel confident establishing group work for design thinking projects.

A second relevant point from research is that, if properly formed and managed, group work in the classroom has potential to mitigate some of the social status issues that show up when students are left to their own social devices. In their book, *Designing Groupwork*, Elizabeth Cohen and Rachel Lotan (2014), developed and documented guidelines for assigning group-worthy tasks and student roles that balance the responsibilities and accountabilities inside groups. These assigned roles help neutralize some of the students' tendencies to grab on to or recede from leadership. It does so by making sure each student in a group makes contributions that are needed. Group members rotate through responsibilities on behalf of the group and each becomes accountable for the group experiences. One piece of advice that Cohen and Lotan propose is that groups or teams are used only for "group-worthy tasks".

This brings us to a third point—that collaborative groups are the necessary lifeblood of design thinking work. Design thinking feeds off of the synergistic energy of the group and having different ways to understand, respond to, and design for a partner is considered an asset. Just as collaboration and team skills are seen as important 21st-century competencies, they are seriously coveted and put into action in design thinking projects. Design thinking challenges will help you cultivate collaborative skills in your students. In design thinking, the group mind and "groupthink" are considered essential and the activities support diverse and multiple contributions.

Given their importance, how might you organize design thinking groups for your classroom activities and projects? There is a why, when, and how for organizing student groups. First, if you have experience in using group work in your classroom, you should rely on that experience. You may already have a comfort zone for forming and managing teams. Our advice is to stick with what has been working for you. If you are new to group work in the classroom, we advise that you spend a bit of time thinking about how you might like to form teams for design projects. You, more than anyone, know your students and your classroom dynamics. This first guideline is about respecting your intuitions. Lotan talks about what she calls "controlled randomness" as a way to form groups. Pick groups out of a hat or use a randomizing program. But then take a look at the results and use your knowledge to separate or put together particular students as you work to balance the groups for meeting students' needs. Randomize, then control for a few of the particulars to ensure high-quality experiences for all. This method and your intuition will get you going.

Second, we have one warning about forming groups. We suggest that you strive for heterogeneous groups and stay completely away from forming ability groups. Grouping by ability could be counterproductive to building students' creative confidence with design thinking and research shows that it is counterproductive in group work. David Kelley and Tom Kelley (of the Stanford d.school and IDEO) define creative competence as "believing in your ability to create change in the world around" (Kelley & Kelley 2013, p. 2). The goal in design thinking is to help every student become an effective problem-solver. We need to be careful to use classroom groups to break through some of the persistent statuses and learning problems we know are at play and that we are already confronting in the classroom. We know it sometimes feels like a leap of faith to think about mixing the students up into heterogeneous groups. Even so, we urge you to do so. We see design thinking exercises as having a low floor and high ceiling, and we believe that all students can enter a challenge where they are and experience the conditions for helping them soar.

We have seen the wisdom of this guideline firsthand. When we worked with a year-round middle school to hold a week-long intersession design thinking camp, 28 students showed up. We facilitators were visitors to the school and on the first day we randomly assigned the students to groups. When the principal was visiting on day three, she remarked how amazed she was at what she saw. When we asked for her to elaborate, she told us that the students were working remarkably well with each other, and students who were usually quiet and uninvolved were quite involved. She then told us that due to uneven recruitment prior to the intersession break, the camp had attracted two subgroups of students—those from the gifted classes and those from the classes for English learners. Practically every student in the room was "classified", but while observing, she could not actually tell who was who in the buzz of activity. She thought that was a much needed, but uncommon achievement on behalf of and for the students. Our naivete about the students' classifications and how they were usually separated in the school ultimately led to new relationships

Exploring the Problem Space

and new kinds of work for them. We think the heterogeneous groups and the nature of design thinking work both contributed. It is the kind of experience we would like to see more often.

With the knowledge that group work will benefit your students socially and academically and with the confidence that you can create heterogeneous groups that are ready to engage and contribute, you will be ready to start design thinking in your classroom.

The Student Design Journal

With your teams set, you are ready to have your students start design thinking activities and challenges. Design thinking activities are varied, yet the activities and ideas that result from them build as students move through the process. We think it is a good idea for students to keep track of their work and progress by documenting their work. We suggest that students of all ages do so in a design journal.

A design journal is a notebook where a designer keeps track of ideas about the design work they are doing. It can contain written notes, sketches, checklists, assignments, and reflections relating to the design project. Professional designers keep design journals, and they can provide students with skill building and a tool that is related to the discipline of design. In the classroom, design journals can be used to help students document their project work and their individual accomplishments or reflections. We have seen design journals used to varying levels of success in classrooms. They can be used like science lab notebooks, sketch books, or diaries. Since designers rely on visuals relating to their work, design journals can be completed even by our youngest students. The learning goals associated with design journaling may include documenting and note keeping, creating visual representations of activity, or even generating new creative ideas. They can involve documentation of feelings, representations of research information, observations, reflections, or ideas.

You can fashion the journaling experience for your students. We have used many kinds of materials for journals. We've had students create paper design journals where teachers gave assignments for students to complete in their journals. We have used folded paper as journals. We have used index cards with holes punched in them and held together with a ring clasp. We have had students keep electronic journals. We have had

33

Four Stages of Design Thinking Process

journals where teachers gave daily reflection or writing assignments and had students compile them in notebooks or folders or binders. We have also seen students in the upper grades take personal and private control over what they recorded or what form their journals took.

During a middle school design camp, we tried out comic book creation as a user-friendly version of journaling (see Figure 1.4 for excerpts from three different comic journals). Our hope was to involve students in chronicling their design activities, generating reflections, and commenting on the STEM-related concepts (Science, Technology, Engineering & Math) involved in their design challenge on access to and conservation of water. Students took photos of their activities each day and then had time to generate their

Figure 1.4 Students document their collaborations in three excerpts from comic journals

(Credit: Shelley Goldman and Molly B. Zielezinski)

individual comic projects. The comics were printed for campers to take home on the last day. Besides providing a take-home product, our goal was to understand what the children captured and produced and to determine if using media technology enhanced the task for the students.

We found that the media-based comics allowed the campers to be extremely expressive and creative while tapping into the design work, their collaborations, and exhibiting knowledge of the STEM-related content of the project (Goldman & Zielezinski 2017). By far, the social experience and group collaboration was most mentioned.

We encourage you to let students use their journals for visual thinking. They can be sketchbooks, visual documentation, places to record reflections, a place to put photos of their projects and a place where they cut photos from other places, to-do lists, and check-off lists of tasks. Journaling may be new to your students, and if it is, you may want to help structure their initial work in their journals. We have been most successful when we have encouraged journaling and given time for it as a legitimate activity, but not treated everything in the journal as an assignment that would be graded. If you do choose to give guidelines, you could leave some choices for students. You might ask them to draw a picture everyday of a project to express their ideas. You can use journals as a place for students to do individual brainstorms, or places to reflect on their designs, group and personal performance. Structure the experience based on what your students might enjoy and the kinds of information and thinking you would like the activity to encompass.

We do recommend that journals attach to accountability. While professional designers might keep their journals personal, often they share them when communicating ideas. In school, most teachers treat the journal more like a lab notebook that gets checked and graded for its contents. Journals may be graded for completeness, the quality of reflections, or how they represent the individual student or groups' points of view. The parameters for how you use and grade journaling will depend on the age and skills of the children.

With experimentation, you can find a balance between treating journals as free-choice, open contributions or as a place for design-related assignments. Too little scaffolding and you might see only empathy journals; too much structure may make them painful for students to complete and take some of the joy out of the design thinking work. Remember the goal is to have students use journals for their ideas and inspirations as much as they are for a record of what they have accomplished.

Four Stages of Design Thinking Process

Figure 1.5 Example of paper-based design journal
(Credit: Saya Iwasaki and Molly B. Zielezinski)

Figure 1.5 is an example for a paper-based journal. The template is simple to use and is available for download at www.routledge.com/ 9780367221331.

Content Connections and Standards

When teaching design thinking, there is also a pedagogical aspect to building background. As a teacher, you need to feel assured that the content and the process involved in your classroom design work is related to what you are indeed supposed to be teaching. This can sometimes be tricky because design projects are much more open-ended than traditional curriculum, which sometimes leaves teachers wondering whether it is fair to claim alignment to standards. If you are a math teacher, for example, it is sometimes hard to be sure whether the students will actually need to engage in standards 2.1, 2.2, and 2.3 to complete the project.

Like when gathering project resources, we encourage teachers to cast a wide net. In terms of content, once you have a scope and sequence for your design lessons (see Chapter 6 for examples), it becomes easier to begin plugging in content standards that are potentially relevant to each phase. While the content standards may vary relative to the problem space, there are standards that you are likely to hit specifically, given the processes students engage with when learning design thinking. In the following sections, we depict the alignment between design thinking processes and the CCSS and the NGSS. In both standards sets, there is ample room for alignment to both the content of a design task and the processes involved in design thinking. For both the CCSS and the NGSS, we will discuss and provide examples of standards alignment to the content and processes involved in design thinking activities. We realize that your state or district may not use these standards as they appear in the documents we cover herein. States and districts have created derivatives of these documents or have developed independent versions of standards or learning progressions and objectives. We look at what is most common and suggest you might interrogate the standards in your district in order to see the correspondences with design thinking.

The Common Core State Standards

The Common Core Standards for Literacy Across the Content Areas (CCSS) privilege specific academic skills such as multiple perspective-taking, the synthesis of information from multiple sources, and in the disciplines, the application of understanding through argumentation and justification. The CCSS "offer a portrait of students who meet the standards set out in this document" (National Governors Association Center for Best Practices & Council of Chief State School Officers 2010a p. 7).

In painting this picture, writers of the standards present seven capacities of college and career readiness in speaking, listening, reading, and writing across the content areas. These capacities are elaborated more specifically within the standards themselves. Our work in schools has shown us that design thinking practices and mindsets have the potential to directly support the development of four of these seven capacities.

Four Stages of Design Thinking Process

Table 1.1 names the four capacities of college and career readiness that are aligned to design thinking, examples of standards that are representative of the capacities, and examples of activities within design thinking that can be used to build students' capacities. Note that Tables 1.1 and 1.2 are adapted from Goldman and Zielezinski (2016).

Next Generation Science Standards

Design thinking also aligns with the NGSS. Our work in design thinking has relevance to many of the disciplinary ideas, crosscutting concepts, and science and engineering practices that are broken down in the NGSS. We find that the disciplinary ideas and cross-cutting concepts are often aligned with the content covered in a design challenge but also that the engineering practices are aligned more globally with the processes involved in design thinking in the classroom. We offer two examples in subsequent text that depict the alignment of design thinking projects to content relevant standards. Next, we offer a crosswalk aligning the engineering practices to the processes involved in design thinking.

Design Thinking and NGSS Content

There are ample grounds to make connections between disciplinary ideas, cross-cutting concepts, and the content covered in various design challenges. Below, we walk you through two specific projects and indicate how each is aligned to NGSS content.

The first example is an international water challenge. The problem space is international water issues. After building background, design teams are each given a user profile (https://docs.google.com/document/d/16PEbxe701h mn88m9g23IZLzWncxjvRr47wQWVjVfhJc/edit) detailing the water-related experiences of someone from another culture. In one profile, tribal leaders from the Xikrin tribe in Brazil give details about their life-damaging conflict with a local company who is polluting their tribal homeland. In another, the struggles of an intergenerational family of farmers from Hyderabad, India are detailed. This first-hand account describes the need for ever-deeper wells as water continues to grow increasingly scarce because of government drilling and water overuse by humans in a climate not suitable for farming.

Both of these reality-based profiles introduce the faces and human perspectives behind the disciplinary core idea in ESS3.C of the NGSS,

Exploring the Problem Space

Table 1.1 Design Thinking in the Common Core State Standards

Capacity for College and Career Readiness	Sample of Standards Aligned to Capacity	Relevant Stage, Tool, or Mindset used in Design Thinking
COMPREHEND AND CRITIQUE *Students are engaged and open-minded—but discerning—readers and listeners. They work diligently to understand precisely what an author or speaker is saying, but they also question an author's or speaker's assumptions and premises and assess the veracity of claims and the soundness of reasoning.* (p. 7)	CCSS.ELA-Literacy.SL.6.1c Pose and respond to specific questions with elaboration and detail by making comments that contribute to the topic, text, or issue under discussion. CCSS.ELA-Literacy.SL.6.4 Present claims and findings, sequencing ideas logically, and using pertinent descriptions, facts, and details to accentuate main ideas or themes. CCSS.ELA-Literacy.WHST.6-8.2d Use precise language and domain-specific vocabulary to inform about or explain the topic.	EMPATHY: ✓ Interviewing ✓ Note-taking during field observations ✓ Note-taking during interviews ✓ Collaborative sharing of notes from observations interviews ✓ Do and say portion of the empathy map. ✓ Capturing user feedback from multiple sources. PROTOTYPE, TEST: ✓ Developing and presenting solutions.
VALUE EVIDENCE *Students cite specific evidence when offering an oral or written interpretation of a text. They use relevant evidence when supporting their own points in writing and speaking, making their reasoning clear to the reader or listener, and they constructively evaluate others' use of evidence.* (p. 7)	CCSS.ELA-Literacy.SL.6.3 Delineate a speaker's argument and specific claims, distinguishing claims that are supported by reasons and evidence from claims that are not. CCSS.ELA-Literacy.WHST.6-8.2b Develop the topic with relevant, well-chosen facts, definitions, concrete details, quotations, or other information and examples. CCSS.ELA-Literacy.W.6.1b Support claim(s) with clear reasons and relevant evidence, using credible sources and demonstrating an understanding of the topic or text.	EMPATHY: ✓ Using do-and-say quadrants of the of empathy map to make inferences recorded in the think and feel quadrants. DEFINE: ✓ Writing and revising point-of-view statements. TEST AND ITERATE: ✓ Collecting user feedback from multiple sources ✓ Iterate on prototype using information from user testing.

(*Continued*)

39

Four Stages of Design Thinking Process

Table 1.1 (Continued))

Capacity for College and Career Readiness	Sample of Standards Aligned to Capacity	Relevant Stage, Tool, or Mindset used in Design Thinking
ESTABLISH KNOWLEDGE BASE *Students establish a base of knowledge across a wide range of subject matter by engaging with works of quality and substance. They become proficient in new areas through research and study. They read purposefully and listen attentively to gain both general knowledge and discipline-specific expertise. They refine and share their knowledge through writing and speaking.* (p. 7)	CCSS.ELA-Literacy.CCRA.W.7 Conduct short as well as more sustained research projects based on focused questions, demonstrating understanding of the subject under investigation. CCSS.ELA-Literacy.CCRA.W.8 Gather relevant information from multiple print and digital sources, assess the credibility and accuracy of each source, and integrate the information while avoiding plagiarism. CCSS.ELA-Literacy.CCRA.W.9 Draw evidence from literary or informational texts to support analysis, reflection, and research.	EMPATHY: ✓ Interviewing ✓ Note-taking during field observations ✓ Note-taking during interviews ✓ Using fiction and non-fiction text as a data source to inform the problem space DEFINE: ✓ Writing and revising point of view statements. IDEATION: ✓ Collaborative brainstorming based on point of view statement PROTOTYPE: ✓ Building low-resolution prototypes to meet a user's need within a problem space TEST AND ITERATE: ✓ Presenting prototypes to users ✓ Gathering feedback from users ✓ Making changes based on feedback

Table 1.1 (Continued)

Capacity for College and Career Readiness	Sample of Standards Aligned to Capacity	Relevant Stage, Tool, or Mindset used in Design Thinking
UNDERSTAND OTHER PERSPECTIVES AND CULTURES *Students appreciate that the twenty-first-century classroom and workplace are settings in which people from often widely divergent cultures and who represent diverse experiences and perspectives must learn and work together. Students actively seek to understand other perspectives and cultures through reading and listening, and they are able to communicate effectively with people of varied backgrounds. They evaluate other points of view critically and constructively. Through reading great classic and contemporary works of literature representative of a variety of periods, cultures, and worldviews, students can vicariously inhabit worlds and have experiences much different than their own.* (p. 7)	CCSS.ELA-Literacy.SL.6.1d Review the key ideas expressed and demonstrate understanding of multiple perspectives through reflection and paraphrasing. CCSS.ELA-Literacy.SL.6.1 Engage effectively in a range of collaborative discussions (one-on-one, in groups, and teacher-led) with diverse partners on grade 6 topics, texts, and issues, building on others' ideas and expressing their own clearly.	Perspective-taking is accomplished not only via addressing this capacity but also as an extension of the each of the capacities & activities presented above. MINDSETS ✓ Perspective-taking through user cantered design. ✓ Perspective-taking through radical collaboration. ✓ Perspective-taking through interviewing and empathy mapping. ✓ Perspective-taking through iteration based on feedback

Note: First two columns are quoted text from the National Governors Association Center for Best Practices & Council of Chief State School Officers (2010b).

Four Stages of Design Thinking Process

Table 1.2 Alignment of Design Thinking Stages and the Next Generation Science Standards

Science and Engineering Practices in NGSS	Relevant Stage and Technique/Tool used in Design Thinking
1. Asking questions (science) and defining problems (engineering)	DEFINE ⇒ Characterizing the user ⇒ Characterizing the needs of a user ⇒ Writing and revising point of view statements
2. Developing and using models	PROTOTYPE ⇒ Building low-resolution prototypes to meet a user's need
3. Planning and carrying out investigations	This occurs when a project covers each stage of the design thinking process and includes some or all components associated with EMPATHY, DEFINE, PROTOTYPE, TEST, ITERATE
4. Analysing and interpreting data	EMPATHY ⇒ Triangulating evidence in "do" and "say" quadrants of empathy map to make inferences recorded in the "think" and "feel" quadrants DEFINE ⇒ Making deep, user-specific inferences explaining tendencies of a particular user by triangulating data collected during empathy phase IDEATION ⇒ Organizing potential solutions into categories ⇒ Rank ordering potential solutions based on specific criteria TEST AND ITERATE: ⇒ Synthesizing feedback gathered during testing ⇒ Engaging in collaborative decision-making about iterations to models and prototypes based on this feedback
5. Using mathematics	N/A

Table 1.2 (Continued)

Science and Engineering Practices in NGSS	Relevant Stage and Technique/Tool used in Design Thinking
6. Constructing explanations (science) and designing solutions (engineering)	**PROTOTYPE** ⇒ Planning for low-resolution prototype ⇒ Building low-resolution prototypes to meet a user's need within a problem space ⇒ Increasing resolution of prototype after numerous feedback-driven iterations
7. Engaging in argument from evidence	**EMPATHY** ⇒ Justifying inferences recorded in the "think" and "feel" quadrants using direct observations recorded in the "say" and "do" column **IDEATION** ⇒ Using point of view statement and evidence from empathy map to identify, discuss, and select most relevant solution(s) to prototype
8. Obtaining, evaluating, and communicating information	**EMPATHY** ⇒ Interviewing and field observations ⇒ Note-taking during field observations and/or interviews ⇒ Collaborative sharing of notes from observations interviews **IDEATION** ⇒ Collaborative brainstorming of hundreds of possible solutions for a problem statement **PROTOTYPE** ⇒ Dialogue supporting collaborative development of prototypes **TEST** ⇒ Presenting prototypes to users, clients, and other design teams ⇒ Collecting user feedback from multiple sources

(https://www.nextgenscience.org/pe/ms-ess3-3-earth-and-human-activity) "typically as human populations and per capita consumption of natural resources increase, so do the negative impacts on the earth unless the activities and technologies involved are engineered otherwise". In this activity, students first define the problem from the perspective of the user, a task that necessitates discussion of specific behaviors and their effects over time on the ecosystem (thus addressing cross-cutting concepts, cause-and-effect, and systems).

In another design task, the water filtration exploration, learners interrogate disciplinary core idea ETS1.B. This standard is explicated in performance expectation MS-LS2-5, (https://www.nextgenscience.org/topic-arrangement/msinterdependent-relationships-ecosystems) which indicates that in covering this standard, learners "Evaluate competing design solutions for maintaining biodiversity and ecosystem services". Water purification, an ecosystem service, is explored as design teams plan, prototype, and test filtration devices that use different combinations of natural materials. As the students compare and evaluate designs within and across teams, they take up a key science and engineering practice: engaging in argument from evidence. Design teams work together to identify the best possible design drawing on evidence recorded during the challenge. This relates to the cross-cutting concept of stability and change as designers have the opportunity to observe first-hand how small differences among purification systems can result in large changes in outcome. Through these and other activities, the STEM- and design thinking-integrated curriculum (https://dloft.stanford.edu/sites/g/files/sbiybj8036/f/dive_in_water_curriculum.pdf) that we created with our REDLab Team at Stanford provides teachers with a proof of concept regarding the application of design thinking to support knowledge development around disciplinary core ideas and cross-cutting concepts in the NGSS.

Design Thinking Processes and Engineering Practices

While uptake of the disciplinary core ideas and cross-cutting concepts is often easy to identify, the strongest alignment between design thinking and the NGSS is definitely in the science and engineering practices listed for each standard. This section of the standards explains broadly what a teacher should do, but there is no elaboration on the methods or pedagogical tools

> ## Science and Engineering Practices
>
> **Asking Questions and Defining Problems**
> Asking questions and defining problems in grades 6–8 builds from grades K–5 experiences and progresses to specifying relationships between variables, and clarifying arguments and models.
> - Ask questions that can be investigated within the scope of the classroom, outdoor environment, and museums and other public facilities with available resources and, when appropriate, frame a hypothesis based on observations and scientific principles. (MS-PS2-3)
>
> **Planning and Carrying Out Investigations**
> Planning and carrying out investigations to answer questions or test solutions to problems in 6–8 builds on K–5 experiences and progresses to include investigations that use multiple variables and provide evidence to support explanations or design solutions.
> - Plan an investigation individually and collaboratively, and in the design: identify independent and dependent variables and controls, what tools are needed to do the gathering, how measurements will be recorded, and how many data are needed to support a claim. (MS-PS2-2)
> - Conduct an investigation and evaluate the experimental design to produce data to serve as the basis for evidence that can meet the goals of the investigation. (MS-PS2-5)

Figure 1.6 Example of science and engineering practices from the Next Generation Science Standards

needed to bring these steps to life. By contrast, our design thinking professional development provides teachers with specific tools, processes, and strategies for building students' capacities to engage in these practices.

Figure 1.6 shows several science and engineering practices that should be used in instruction of the Motion and Stability standards for middle school students. The first, asking questions and defining problems, indicates that teachers should have students ask questions that can be answered in local contexts and, if appropriate, follow up with observations and hypotheses. This leaves a reader wondering exactly how this is done. You cannot just tell a middle school student to go out and ask answerable questions. The process and mindsets utilized in design thinking provide teachers with a set of tools, strategies, and coaching techniques for this and other engineering practices. These processes and mindsets will be elaborated in the coming chapters.

These practices are addressed in the international water challenge and filtration exploration described above. In the coming chapters, we offer the tools that you will need to facilitate design thinking challenges. These include multi-step processes for developing context-specific problem statements. We also offer a clear approach to coach students toward asking answerable questions and defining problems.

Since the engineering practices in the NGSS and the design thinking process are each informed to some degree by the engineering design process, the relevance of our tools is not restricted to asking questions. Various techniques are introduced for each phase of a design challenge, and given this variety in method, teachers can access a robust pedagogical toolkit for teaching these practices. (See Table 1.2 for additional information about the link between design thinking and the NGSS Science and Engineering Practices.)

We do not contend that our tools are the only ones that can be used to accomplish the engineering practices, only that they are suitable, contain sufficient detail to be actionable, and can be used flexibly (as a collective set or one at a time as needed). By sharing some examples, we are drawing attention to the applicability of design thinking to the new standards. Furthermore, we are making the claim that the inclusion of science and engineering practices in the NGSS provides a warrant for the use of design thinking and alignment details as evidence that design thinking is a highly relevant process for the teaching of both the CCSS and NGSS. Teachers, often exhilarated by the tools we offer, can see the CCSS and NGSS as opening the door for applying design thinking in service of the new standards.

References

Achieve, Inc. (2013). *Next Generation Science Standards. On behalf of the twenty-six states and partners that collaborated on the NGSS*. Washington, DC: The National Academies Press.

Cohen, E. G. (1994). Restructuring the classroom: Conditions for productive small groups. *Review of Educational Research Spring 1994*, 64(1), 1–35.

Cohen, E. G., & Lotan, R. A. (2014). *Designing groupwork: Strategies for the heterogeneous classroom third edition*. Teachers College Press.

Davidson, N. (2021). Introduction to Pioneering Perspectives in Cooperative Learning. In N. Davidson (Ed.), *Pioneering perspectives in cooperative learning: Theory, research, and practice in diverse approaches to CL*. New York, NY, Routledge.

Goldman, S., & Zielezinski, M. B. (2016). Teaching with Design Thinking: Developing New Vision and Approaches to Twenty-First-Century Learning. In *Connecting science and engineering education practices in meaningful ways* (pp. 237–262). Cham: Springer.

Goldman, S., & Zielezinski, M. B. (2017). The Production of Learning Stories Through Comic Making. In M. Núñez-Janes, A. Thornburg, & A. Booker (Eds.), *Deep stories: Practicing, teaching, and learning anthropology with digital storytelling* (pp. 36–59). Warsaw: DeGruyter Open.

Kelley, T., & Kelley, D. (2013). *Creative confidence: Unleashing the creative potential within us all*. Currency.

National Governors Association Center for Best Practices & Council of Chief State School Officers (2010a). *Common core state standards*. Washington, DC: National Governors Association Center for Best Practices & Council of Chief State School Officers.

National Governors Association Center for Best Practices & Council of Chief State School Officers (2010b). *Common core state standards for English language arts and literacy in history/social studies, science, and technical subjects*. Washington, DC: National Governors Association Center for Best Practices & Council of Chief State School Officers.

2 | Empathizing

Figure 2.1
(Credit: Saya Iwasaki)

Why Empathy in Design Thinking?

In July of 2018, the world watched as a team of 12 boys and their coach were located after being stranded deep inside a cave in Thailand. Plans for keeping them safe and their rescue were needed.

The world watched as all kinds of experts were called in to help with the emergency. It was a precarious and dangerous situation in every way. Ultimately, all the boys and their coach were saved, although one experienced diver who was trying to deliver oxygen tanks was not.

We retell this story to show how the rescue operation was handled with an empathy approach. Every decision or part of the plan was completely dependent on the state of the boys who were stranded. Did they know how to swim? Were they strong enough? Were they healthy enough or energetic

Empathizing

enough after being stranded? Would they be scared to be underwater and breathing through full masks, and when they had to squeeze through a space 15 inches wide (38.1 cm), how would they react?

Many solutions were considered. One idea was to drill a hole through the mountain into the chamber and lift them out. Another was to send in a mini-submarine. They eventually decided to use secured safety lines, multiple divers for the rescue of each child so they could be guided out one by one and could rest along the way. Ultimately the decisions behind the rescue plans were all made because it was what could work for the boys. That was a quintessential design thinking solution—one that was conceived based on the needs of the persons for whom they were creating the solution. The solution was low-tech and people-intensive. It turned out to be the solution that was based on careful assessment of the boys' needs and gave the experts confidence that they could keep them physically and emotionally safe while moving them through the flooded cave. The rescue of the team was completely successful. A lot of thinking and problem-solving went into coming up with the final solution.

Empathy is the capacity to step into the shoes of another and see the world from their perspective. It can be described as a meeting of head and heart. The empathy mandate of design thinking refers to the many methods of capturing, observing, engaging with, and immersing oneself in the perspectives and livelihoods of others and making them central in the process. The empathy work we do in design thinking not only puts the "human" in human-centered design, it also asserts that complex problems are not only technical in nature but have equally complex social and real-world dimensions to them. That was certainly true in the case of the soccer team rescue.

In the rescue, it was obvious that the design of the plan was in complete consideration of the boys. Of course, they needed to be at the center. Putting humans first was absolutely essential to rescuing them. Design thinking generalizes this attention to human needs and perspectives and relies on empathy even when the design is of an object, a product, or a process. In all design cases, empathy is central. Whether we are designing a new technology, a new way to teach, or a new event or process for our community, empathy should be at the center. As we move through the world, we encounter the results of poor designs that did not take their human users into consideration—from door handles that are difficult to open to tools made for people who are only right-handed or to lines we

Four Stages of Design Thinking Process

wait in at airports that leave us tired or impatient. We wonder, "What were they thinking"? It's reasonable to think that those who create the designed world should have considered us. This act of working from a position of empathy is a pillar of design thinking.

In this chapter, we take you through an exploration of empathy work in design thinking. We will tell stories about empathy and suggest activities for you to exercise empathy and bring it into classroom activities with your students. We will also move through the empathy process so you can see how we exercise empathy and mine it to define the solution possibilities when inside a design thinking project. The work we do to develop empathy and then apply it in the design process is a key feature of the design work. We always want to couple its importance with how important and helpful empathy is to the enterprise of growing young hearts and minds. Empathy work enables us to sense and understand other people's emotions, learn about the ways they think and act, and even to understand how and why they act as they do at certain times or under particular conditions. As educators, we deeply believe that teaching students to learn about, train for, and then put empathy to work when they are engaged in thinking, problem-solving, design work, making, and play, leads them to become more connected persons, learners, and classroom community members. Hopefully, as you read, you will see how integrated empathy is to both the design process and the general education enterprise.

We view empathy as a big part of the human endeavor. The Dalai Lama is attributed with saying, "Love and compassion are necessities, not luxuries. Without them humanity cannot survive". It is a lofty ideal to put empathy for K-12 teachers and students with the grand challenges to humanity, yet empathy is increasingly recognized for its role in work and community settings. So, what can we learn about the role empathy might play inside your classrooms?

We know that empathy can be a deep feature of social and human development and a method for content learning that might be a brain changer and therefore a classroom game changer. We see empathy completely consistent with educating K-12 students and see it as a complementary partner to the intellectual work we ask students to do. It is another dimension for our students' learning and growth. In his 2006 TED Talk about creativity in education (https://www.ted.com/talks/sir_ken_robinson_do_schools_kill_creativity), the late Sir Ken Robinson, an education writer and critic, mused about how we "educate our students from the waist up". In his talks, he strove to show how we need to take care of other centers of human thought, creativity, and brilliance. We agree. When students are working from a place of empathy, they are motivated, considerate, kind, and most of all, committed to those for whom they are designing. We like to think they are in partnership with the others as they are problem-solving. When we see a child acting empathetically, we see the best of their humanity in action. As teachers, we see this as a thing of beauty as well as a key driver of learning.

There are a few points to keep in mind about empathy in the K-12 classroom:

1. **The importance of empathy as a human capacity is widely recognized and we know it can be learned, cultivated, and put into action.** Through experiments and documentation of many situations and cases where empathy is expressed, research has shown that empathy is "real". The research has shown the unique ways that the brain reacts during empathy. In his book, *Social: Why our Brains Are Wired to Connect*, Matthew D. Lieberman writes about our social brains. He discusses empathy, saying that "empathy is a more complex process that serves to get us ready to help others" (p. 152). Lieberman reviews some of the research that established empathy as activity in the brain. He explains the study by Tania Singer in England that showed in experiments that women's brains registered pain when they thought their boyfriends were being shocked (Lieberman 2013; Singer et al. 2004). He points out that "Empathy is arguably the pinnacle of our social cognitive achievements. It requires us to understand the inner emotional worlds of other people and then act in ways that benefit other people and our relationships with them" (p. 160). While people are probably born with a natural capacity for empathy, we have learned that it can be developed. In the book, *The Emotional Life of Your Brain: How Its Unique Patterns Affect the Way You Think, Feel, and Live–and How You Can Change Them*, Davidson and Begley (2013) describe the connections between brain and heart and discuss studies that show how empathy must and can be trained and practiced. Being empathetic and acting with empathy takes training. When we work with the Stanford d.school staff, they orient to the importance and centrality of empathy in the

design thinking process, and they describe and treat empathy as a "muscle" that can be exercised and developed. We like this idea and metaphor. In our design thinking work, we have always made empathy a centerpiece of the process with educators and students, and in doing so, we have witnessed many powerful instances of empathy and empathy put into action through the exercise of positive design work. Empathy is both a component of the design thinking process and a mindset further developed through design thinking work.

2. **Empathy development is completely compatible with work we do with students in K-12 education.** Empathy is social and emotional in nature, but it can be a good companion to the cognitive and social growth and achievement we want to see for our students. We see it in design thinking activities and we also see it integrated into social and emotional learning and equity work that is being addressed more and more in our classrooms and schools. In an article in Edutopia (November 11, 2015) about how she took a year to focus her curriculum around empathy, teacher Laura Owen points out that empathy builds positive classroom culture, strengthens community, and prepares students to become leaders in their communities. We also look to the country of Denmark where K-12 students receive an empathy curriculum once a week. There, empathy is considered essential to educating happy students and happy citizens who can work collaboratively and take care of others (Alexander & Sandahl, 2014). In the United States, we orient unevenly in the standards, goals, and curricula to social and emotional learning and its importance in the learning process, with empathy being one aspect of the social and emotional learning palette. We obviously would like to see more attention to the role that empathy can play and we are delighted that design thinking can bring empathy work into the classroom.

3. **Empathy enables us to design solutions to problems with greater clarity about people and their circumstances.** Empathy work can help us see where people are rubbing up against constraints of the system and help us design with advocacy. As part of a research project, we were invited to study the process of school-based design thinking teams in the San Francisco Unified School

District (SFUSD). The district was using design thinking as a vehicle for designing new programs and structures for increasing students' educational access, equity, and success. (See a full description at https://www.sfusd.edu/departments/ilab.) On pitch night for projects, we heard team after team report that they saw their students and communities in new ways after implementing a series of empathy exercises. Some teams interviewed their community members, others observed, administered surveys, held focus groups, or created prototypes for stimulating community conversation and feedback. Their empathy insights led them to devise and propose new design projects as improvements at their school sites (for example, a new teacher center, a high school course on the history of Black women, a leadership program instead of suspensions for elementary boys, and a community welcome lounge). During the pitches, emotions around empathy ran high, and they were clearly motivating the teams to move forward towards implementation of new designs. It was powerful to us that design thinking, empathy work, and the hard tasks of addressing equity could have so much synergy. We are inspired by those SFUSD teams, who committed to an empathy-driven process because we believe it was part of helping them disrupt long-standing inequities and create alternative opportunities through design. One idea of what is called "liberatory design" is to shift the relationships between those who hold the power to design and those who are impacted by them, and to use design to increase critical learning and increased agency for designers. The empathy process is a major place where this equalizing work is rooted. As you can tell, we are advocates for employing design thinking for accomplishing equity work in classrooms, schools, and districts.

We continually advocate for empathy as part of K-12 education. We aspire to leverage the empathy work you do inside the classroom community, and apply and strengthen it in design thinking challenges. Empathy is a key and powerful driver of design thinking, and applying it in projects will have effects that may last students a lifetime. We suggest you start by doing a small bit of empathy work yourself or with a small group of colleagues.

Four Stages of Design Thinking Process

In the next section, we take time with an example of empathy at work with a list of exercises you can use to explore your own capacity for empathy at work.

Start with an Empathy Exercise

We start with empathy exercises that you can complete to boot or reboot your empathy engines. You might like to start by sitting quietly and answering the following questions:

Exercise 1: ask yourself one of the following questions and reflect on how you would like to exercise your empathy.

- Have I missed being truly empathetic with any of my students? Is there more that I could learn about them?
- I am naturally empathetic. Could I learn to more effectively put my empathy to work with my students?

Once you have answered the questions, you can start to engage some empathy processes. There are many ways to gather information and insights in an empathy process. We concentrate on observation and interviews because they are common in many design thinking projects. You can do these at school or even as online events. While we realize it might be difficult to accomplish them while you are teaching, you might observe a student at an elective or specialty class during your prep or at lunch or playground time. Or, you might be able to ask another teacher or administrator to "cover" your class one time so you can observe or interview. You will learn a lot even if you only observe or interview for 15–30 minutes.

Exercise 2: observe a student. Prepare by writing down three ideas or conceptions you have about the student. Then observe. Notice the student's behaviors and actions. Take notes on what you see. Write down as many notes as you can, trying to stick to descriptions of what you see. When looking at your notes, ask what you noticed about the student? Did you see anything that was different from your "usual" observations? Summarize your feelings about the student after the observation.

Add to your empathy experiences by interviewing a student or calling their parent(s)/guardian(s) as a way to get to know them better. Make sure to let them describe their child to you. What do they see as the child's

Empathizing

strengths or challenges? Again, take notes. Take the time to note what you have noticed or learned about the student. Try to reflect on and strive for a new learning for you about the student.

Exercise 3: interview a co-teacher or an administrator in your school. Ask them to describe their day, their favorite activities, and the things that make them most stressed. What do they think might make their jobs better? If they could make one change in their school with a magic wand, what would it be? Ask for many details on their stories. You can share, but mostly get them sharing. Take notes. Reflect on what mattered the most to your colleague. What are their hopes and dreams? What are their biggest stressors?

If you complete one or more of these activities, you will start your empathy engines. You might already be thinking about how you can help or create ways to make life better. Experiencing empathy and wanting to put those feelings to work will help you become a better design thinker.

We outline one more activity that will engage you in an empathy experience for a student and also give you the chance to put your empathy to work.

Exercise 4: we ask you to focus your interactions, observations, thoughts, and assessments on one student who might be concerning you or is in need of some additional attention or resources. This student will be your inspiration (similar to when your students work with a design partner, yet for this exercise, one step away since you will not be engaging the student directly). The goal of the activity is to have you focus on the student with empathy, try out an empathy process, and represent your understanding of the child in a physical representation. The physical representation will be a reminder of your insights about that student as you plan lessons, activities, and future interactions for the student. The representation will be a 2D or 3D creation. It could be a likeness of the student or an abstraction. It could be a doll, a puppet, a spirit animal, a flag, or an environment that represents the student when they are most comfortable.

Ultimately, you can place your product of the student in view when you plan for your class sessions. Then, ask the question, "How can I plan this activity to make the environment conducive to this student's dispositions and needs"? Let's say you decide that your student's spirit animal is a bear, you can ask yourself, "How do I design to keep a bear best participating in this activity"? You will have different responses if your student is more like an ostrich. Then you might ask, "How do I design to keep their head out of the sand"? If your student is distracted by noise, you might ask, "How might I incorporate a quiet place to work"?

Activity Plan: Exercise Your Empathy Muscles

Preparation

Choose a student in your class to inspire this empathy work. Choose one who might benefit from your concentration and efforts on their behalf or one who has been on your mind recently.

Materials

- Gather prototyping materials (see prototyping list pages 99–100).
- "Needs/Strengths/Solutions" table in this lesson's Resources section

Activity Overview

You will build empathy and need-finding skills. You will organize information, impressions, observations, and insights, and then represent them by creating a physical representation of the student. This exercise will help you identify the students' strengths and needs. You can place the physical model near where you do your thinking and planning (your ongoing design thinking work) to remind you of the student when you do.

Learning Objectives

Participants will:

- Gather information and ideas they have about the student
- Reflect on what has been gathered and choose a few important points
- Create a model that is a representation of the student (build a prototype)
- Create a needs statement to accompany the model
- Create a classroom/school experience that incorporates the student's needs and strengths

Empathizing

Steps for the Activity

Step 1: choose your student. Use your paper, whiteboard, or sticky notes to generate a four-column list. Label the columns for Strengths, Challenges, Needs, and Does Best When (see Figure 2.2 for alternative whiteboard setup for this activity).

Step 2: spend some time filling out the chart. You might get information for the chart from several sources. You might consult some of the student's works or assignments. If you are in the school year, you might observe the student in the next few days and record some of their behaviors. You can retrieve information from your experiences with the child inside or outside of the classroom and include anything you might know from other people including other teachers, the child's parents or family members. Think about what you know the student loves to do or excels at and try to understand the structure of that activity or interest in case you can find a way to the student through it.

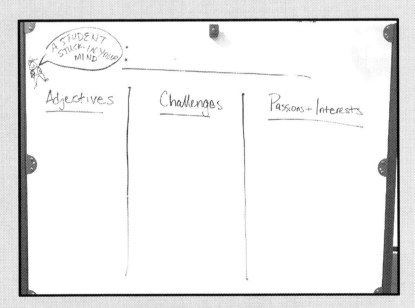

Figure 2.2 Example set-up for step 1 of teacher empathy exercise (Credit: Shelley Goldman)

Four Stages of Design Thinking Process

Step 3: create a statement that expresses your point of view (PoV) concerning the student. For this empathy activity, use the following form:

*To be successful in my classroom, _____,
needs a way*

to_____

by _____.

A couple of examples of PoV statements that other teachers have written for this activity include:

A highly distractible, made fun of, brilliantly artistic 6th grader, Julian, needs a way to focus his energy towards success in math by channeling and using his artistic qualities.

Super social, chatty, disorganized, and often late on assignments Serena needs a way to work with others so she can harness her social energy towards classroom tasks by working with a natural sense of accountability among her classroom teams.

Step 4: use prototyping materials to create a representation of your student that shows the student's strengths or challenges. This representation will be an artifact of your empathy activity and can be used as a reminder of the student's strengths and challenges. You can see some examples in Figure 2.3.

Step 5: design a lesson or experience for the student based on the needs statement and what you included in your representation of the student.

Now is the time to think more concretely about what you might design for this student in the classroom. Put your empathy into action by trying one or more of the suggestions that follow.

Suggestions:

- Choose at least two passions, interests, or strengths of your student. Think of how you might construct an activity for this child based on these assets?
- Choose one or two Challenges from your empathy chart. Can you match them with one of the Strengths/passions? Can you think of how to structure an activity or set of activities based on them?

Empathizing

Figure 2.3 Photos of teacher representations of students
(Credit: Shelley Goldman)

Step 6: congratulate yourself! You have just practiced empathy and designed a lesson or an experience based on it.

Empathy in the Classroom

Now that you have experienced one or more exercises in empathy, it is time to turn your attention to how to bring empathy work into your classroom. We show how empathy grounds design thinking through the story of

Four Stages of Design Thinking Process

9th graders who engaged in a multiple school design thinking challenge. The story and the lessons we learned from their experiences about how empathy is the bedrock for K-12 design thinking are followed by a section that takes you through some tools, exercises, and steps for working with your students on empathy.

The Patient Comfort Challenge

We arranged an off-site, three-day design challenge with our collaborators in Utah. On a Monday morning, 9th-grade student design teams from three Salt Lake City high schools were brought together for a design thinking challenge at a highly interactive and experiential local museum. The students were joined by industry designers who make patient medical devices as well as people who had recently been patients or taken care of patients with serious illnesses who had interacted with various medical devices. The students were presented with a challenge to transform the meaning of patient comfort for people with serious medical conditions.

The museum offered some opportunities for building background, so each student team started the day with introductions and improv exercises as a way to break the ice and build some team spirit. They were introduced to the patient comfort challenge and immediately asked to gather some thoughts about patient care from museum-goers. Each team created a question or two about patient care and wrote them on large whiteboards that they placed in various locations on the museum floor. One group asked, "What would you want for your child if you were in the emergency room"? and "What bothers your child when they go to the hospital"? While the whiteboards were sitting out on the museum floor, the teams were introduced to interviewing techniques, and after preparing interview questions and roles, conducted two important interviews for building background and building empathy. The first interview was with a representative from the biotechnology company that makes medical devices such as shunts and stents. They discussed what they make, their design and development processes, and their interactions with their users—the patients. These interviews were about the technology development process and were designed to help the students develop background. They were informational, and there was note-taking, questions, and some slides to see about the different devices.

Empathizing

Next, the student teams moved to working with their design partners. These were the people that would be the focus of the empathy process and the resulting designs. They would inspire the design and later provide feedback. One partner was a current patient, one was a family caregiver of his deceased father, and third was a hospice worker who took care of patients at the end of their lives. These interviews took a different tone. Notepads were put down. The design partners told stories about how they or their patients coped with what they went through. These were deeply serious and personal conversations. Some of the students and the partners cried. All three groups went more than an hour over the time that had originally been allotted for the interviews. Goodbyes were said, although each team would see their design partners once again later when it was time for feedback on design direction and a prototype.

After lunch, we guided the student teams through conversations and exercises to help them harness their empathy for their design partners and realize insights based on what they had learned. Each team created an empathy chart that helped them retrieve and visually organize some of the information about their partner and get it into bite-sized bits. The purpose of the empathy charts was to help capture and visualize what was learned from and about the design partners and gave students a way to visualize and deal with all the different kinds of information, ideas, and insights they had at hand (see example empathy chart in Figure 2.4). This helped them separate descriptions and interpretations of what the design partner "said" and "did" from their interpretations and descriptions of the person, although it enabled them to make a record of both. They also completed a needs analysis based on what they heard from their client by answering the question, "Our partner expressed or inferred these needs"? Once these activities were done, we asked them to discuss and highlight the needs they saw as most relevant to their design partner and also describe the partner. The empathy process continued into the crafting of a PoV statement that ultimately directed the inspiration and focus for the rest of their design project.

Once each group had a focus and PoV for their design, they moved on to the next stage of the process—brainstorming and prototyping work. Each group generated 50 or more ideas for solutions, ranked them, chose one, and began to create prototypes. At the end of the second day, their design partners returned to the museum to experience the prototypes and give feedback. One design partner was given a walk-through of a room-sized

Four Stages of Design Thinking Process

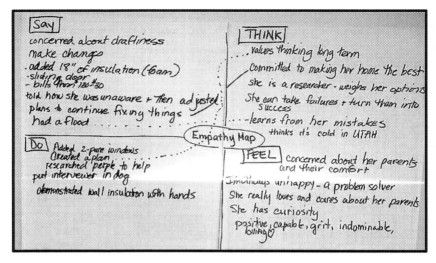

Figure 2.4 An empathy chart after a home energy interview (Credit: Shelley Goldman)

model of a new concept for chemotherapy centers that accommodates patients, relatives, and friends, and included a smoothie bar and lessons about cooking during chemotherapy. Another client, a son who took care of his ailing father, was able to try a prototype of a life-sized portable, roll-in shower equipped with heated floors and towels that could have helped his father stay extra warm. The third client, a hospice caretaker for cancer patients, was presented a high-tech hospital room with a wall for video-calls, a display area for messaging with family and friends, and a touch-screen patient schedule to help patients keep track of their tests and treatments and keep their family members informed.

All three design partners were moved by the sensitivity of the students to their needs, the brilliance of the prototypes, and the ingenuity of the teams. They each saw that their concerns were heard and that the solutions the teams generated connected so deeply with what they had shared. They offered feedback.

The students listened intently and once again engaged in revisions before the final presentations the next evening to teachers, family, friends, and their principals. The students and their teachers left the project thinking they should continue their work. At a final presentation of their projects back at school, one boy said he thought he'd come to the challenge for one day just to get out of classes, but initially planned to not return. When he

Empathizing

spoke during the presentations, he said he just knew he could not abandon his team's design partner because she really was dealing with a lot. He said, "I did it for her".

This student's statement revealed the crux of how empathy works in the design process. It pushes the "start" button and gives meaning to the design work. The empathy imperative is always present and underlies and inspires all design decisions that go forward. When the student teams finished the design thinking challenge, the solutions spoke directly to the patients' comfort.

While there is much to learn from this story of design thinking with students, we tell it to show how empathy drove this student design challenge. While hearing about and concentrating on design work about ill patients was a compelling topic, it alone did not necessarily give students the ability to identify and use their empathy in focused and productive ways in the design thinking process. Us teachers and facilitators constructed an experience that would let students feel empathy and we helped them to process their raw empathy, gain insights from it, and then to focus around it during the solution-oriented phases of the design challenge.

Everyone involved in the patient comfort challenge was touched by how empathy drove the challenge. The work put into empathy in the patient comfort challenge did more than just provide the engine for the design process and solutions. The empathy work that the students accomplished enabled them to have deep and intense collaborations with each other, their design partners, their teacher, and us facilitators. When the teams demonstrated their designs, all that were present recognized the students' motivations and contributions—and many wept. One principal begged the students to start working with him immediately to design their school so students would not want to drop out. Shortly after, several middle schools in the city decided to introduce design thinking to 8th-grade students, and the newly minted, 9th-grade design thinkers were asked to be coaches for the younger students. For the students, different connections were made with peers, adults, and content topics of interest to them. The challenge also built their confidence.

The empathy experience of the student team members reminds us of how powerful empathy can be when it is put to good use. Empathy probably drives some of what we do in our classrooms every day, and with design thinking, we can harness it to open the doors of the classroom to life, its challenges, and to learn that is truly transformative and impactful.

The solutions in the patient challenge spoke directly to the needs of the design partners. They were sophisticated enough solutions that biotech company partners were quite impressed and considered how they might help these student solutions come into reality. There was no doubt for any of the teachers and adults present that what drove the work was the empathy the students developed and how that empathy was the inspiration for each of the solutions. Situating empathy work inside a design thinking challenge can really make it an effective project driver and can also impact students' efficacy as designers and people in the world who can respond to others' needs.

Tools and Activities for Classroom Empathy Work

A design thinking exercise as complex as the patient comfort challenge may seem like a tall order, but it illustrates some of the ways that you can begin to work with your students to bring empathy front and center inside your classroom. Accomplishing empathy work is consistent with many of the academic skills you will be working on with your students, such as researching, interviewing, observing, documenting, and interpreting information. It also taps into the 21st-century skills such as collaborating, working creatively, problem-solving, and communicating (see Table 1.2 in Chapter 1 for examples of how these skills are found in national standards documents). We suggest you can start out with confidence that the time you invest on empathy work is attending to both social and academic skills. We share a few ways you can get started in exercising empathy with your students.

We suggest you start by teaching your students the empathy process using one of two methods. The first is to employ an interview. The second is to try a character-centered empathy process, wherein your students work on empathy for the characters in stories or passages. We have used both of these techniques effectively. We explain each and give you activity guidelines for using them with your students. We also give mention to additional free empathy activities we have used. After spending time on interviews and character study methods, we introduce tools and resources for extrapolating insights from the empathy methods.

Method 1: Empathy Through Interviewing

To start working on empathy through an interview activity, your students will need to be matched with a design partner. The design partners will be the person they get to know, interview, work through empathy exercises with, and focus on as the end-users of their eventual designs. There are many people that can be enlisted as design partners for a class interviewing process. Other students in the school or the class, teachers and other staff in the school, and family or community members can all be powerful interview partners for students. Who you choose will be dependent on other goals you may want to accomplish as part of any empathy activity.

Once you decide who your students will interview, it is time for the students to prepare interview questions. You may want to give them a topic for their interviews (see Chapter 1 for backgrounding), and have a lesson or two about the kinds of questions that may be developed. Topics for interviews can be very focused (e.g., we want to know when and what you eat for breakfast) or very open (e.g., we want to know about your childhood). You can have the generation of interview questions be a highly structured whole-class activity or you might let students come up with their own questions more independently and help them hone them through feedback and revision. You want the students to avoid questions that have yes or no answers. You will want to make sure that the students develop questions that will elicit rich descriptions and stories from their interview partners.

Interview Guidelines

Here are the rules for interviewing that we provide to our students:

1. **Be prepared**. Decide some questions ahead of time. You can ask questions during the interview as they come to mind, but it is best to have enough prepared questions.
2. **Value the time**. Be on time. Offer to end when the time allotted is up.
3. Greet your design partner and tell them what you will be doing.
4. **Make sure to listen**. Repeat back what you hear. Make eye contact. Ask follow-up questions about what your design partner

seems to care about. You can say, "Can you tell me more about..."?
5. **Go for specific questions**. Ask your design partner to tell stories. Or describe their activities.
6. **Be thankful**. Thank your design partner. Tell them you would like to show them your eventual prototype if they were willing to see it and give you feedback.

Bad Interviewing Practices and How to Avoid Them

Sometimes, it is helpful to let students identify bad interviewing techniques or behaviors. Some that we expect students to be able to describe and avoid are:

1. **Phones**: leaving them or their ringers on, taking a call, or looking at a text.
2. **Coming unprepared**: not having questions prepared; not being able to explain your greater design challenge; not having decided who interviews or how you will take turns, who takes notes; and forgetting your note-making materials.
3. **Not respecting your design partner**: do not be distracted, do not seem bored, do not interrupt, and do not judge your design partner or speak out when you disagree.

Processing the Empathy Interviews

When interviews are completed, you will want your students to fill out the notes they were able to take. Make sure they have the time for this activity. They might answer some questions such as:

1. **Describe your design partner**. Let them know they should use as many words to describe their design partners as they can. They can be factual and interpretive in these descriptions because it will help them get their thoughts together. You might have to get the students to find as many positive words to describe their design partner as negative words. We like to push on the positive descriptors to open up some of the doors of empathy.
2. What was the most surprising story you heard? Write down as much of it as you can.

3. What does your design partner care about?
4. What upsets or frustrates your design partner?
5. What are they hoping for?

Once your students have prepared for interviews, conducted them, and reflected on them, your students will be ready to start exercising their empathy for insights about their design partners and choosing a focus for the rest of their design project.

Method 2: Empathy Exercises from Characters

Besides interviewing, we have found it useful and productive to use character studies from books and literature helpful in growing empathy skills. There are many opportunities for your students to focus on empathy that depend on the grade and subjects you teach. We suggest a short empathy exercise that you can do in class around a character in a reading or a character who is an historical or cultural influencer in your subject or discipline. This short activity will involve students drawing character descriptions and starting to reflect on character's ideas, dilemmas, or needs.

Activity Plan: The Story Character Challenge for Student Empathy Development (K-2)

Preparation

Choose a book or article you will be reading with the class to inspire this empathy activity. Use a book that has one or more compelling characters who meet with a dilemma. The characters can be fictional or real-life. We worked with a teacher who did this activity brilliantly with Kindergarten students using the fairy tale, *Cinderella*. You can use readings from your curriculum, popular books, or even popular online pieces about influential artists, historians, scientists, mathematicians, cultural icons, etc.

Materials

- Reading materials
- Blank empathy chart

Lesson Overview

In this activity, the students will read and then build empathy. They will complete an empathy chart for one of the characters.

Learning Objectives

Students will:

- Listen to or read a story, part of a story, or a biographical description
- Show they understand a character in the story
- Identify needs, issues, or dilemmas of the character.

Activities

Step 1: read a story or profile (or part of a story) with the class. You may want them to have them listen to the story if they are pre-readers or young readers. They read on their own if they are older (yet we always still read regularly to our middle-school students). If there is more than one character, discuss each character briefly. Divide the students into groups to study one of the characters.

Step 2: understand the character and identify the character's needs. In this step, groups identify characteristics and predicaments of their characters. In the early grades, you may work on one character at a time so you can talk through and record information with the students. In the upper grades you may want the students to independently explore their characters. Each group returns to the text and tries to gather as much information about the character as they can. Once they go through the text, they can act at a more interpretive level, adding their ideas and inferences about their character. They can list information they gather. It's also good to have them create a list of adjectives that describe their character.

Empathizing

> Have them respond to a sampling of the following questions:
>
> - Words that describe your character.
> - What helped them resolve their story?
> - What feelings or issues was the character experiencing and grappling with?
> - What do you think the character needs? Does the character have goals? Problems?
> - What actions did your character take? What did they do?
> - What did your character say that was important?

Additional Methods for Generating Empathy

There are additional ways to generate empathy insights. We show a three-column chart later in this chapter that we use alongside empathy charts as a scaffold to create a focus for the next steps in the design process. We complete multiple rounds of empathy charting and have young designers try different ways to express their empathy insights. Four that we have been successful with include:

1. **Full-body empathy chart**. On a large piece of butcher block paper roll, use a marker to trace the outline of a person. Then fill the insides with all the information, ideas, feelings about the design partner's emotions. Maybe surround the paper outside the body with topics or ideas or people with whom the partner connects.
2. **Portraits of design partners**. After empathy charts, we sometimes ask our students to create original portraits of their design partners (with surroundings if they choose). We think of these as original artworks that capture the essence of the design partner. You can make media available and let students create their portraits; you can also limit media and materials and styles of portraits based on other learning objectives you are trying to accomplish.
3. **Dioramas**. Students can create dioramas that show their design partners in a scene or space from their lives based on what they

described for the students. Shoe boxes work well as homes for dioramas.

4. **Comic representations**. As we mentioned, we had students create comics using available software. This can be facilitated if student designers have access to photos of their interviewees.

Tools for Generating Empathy Insights

The Empathy Chart

Once you and your students engage in empathy work, you will want some tools you can rely on to help them gain insights from their interviews. The tool we use the most is the empathy chart. An empathy chart lets designers record their notes about a design partner in a visual format so they can see them all in one place. It also organizes the notes so they can be mined and brought front and center in the design work. It can help the designers separate what is describable behavior of the interviewee—what they said and what they said they thought or felt. It can also include a few interpretations that the designers had about what the person thought and felt.

In an empathy chart, we create a number of sections and post relevant notes and impressions in the sections. The most frequently used empathy charts divide into quadrants that are labeled to answer the questions, "What does your partner *Do, Say, Think, & Feel*"? Figure 2.4 is an example of a common empathy chart and the way it was organized and filled in after a short interview with a partner about home energy habits and issues.

From Empathy to Defining a Focus for Solutions

Using the character study as an empathy exercise is a good way to introduce empathy work into your classroom. We have now looked at both character studies and interviews. Empathy can be exercised and developed by observing as well. Students can observe others in classes or events around the school and take notes on how people are behaving in them. They can shadow a person for a period of time or over several sessions. In one school, the students observed students over lunch periods. In another, they watched the person leading the school parking and pick up at the end of a school day. We have discussed how surveys, focus groups, and prototypes have been used in developing empathy. You can choose any of these ways to help your students gather information from design partners as part of empathy work. They each will help provide your students with the practice they need to develop new emapthy skills. We share a few guidelines for empathy interviewing because it is the most frequently invoked empathy method in K-12 design thinking situations. These guidelines may seem obvious to you, and it is good if they do. They are also discoverable inside a short activity that you can do with students in your classroom. We assure you that they will be both fun and a challenge for your students to accomplish.

In each case, the students were listening, watching, taking notes, and then organizing them on an empathy chart.

As it turns out, the empathy chart is only the first step in exercising empathy. To make use of empathy in the design thinking process, we need to be more strategic with generating the insights that empathy work can yield. Getting from the empathy chart to insights and then to focused problem-solving is the goal.

In this section, we discuss drawing insights from design partners in ways that can focus your classroom design work. Interrogating the empathy chart and prioritizing a few key insights makes it easier to define a focal direction for the solutions space. This stage of empathy work—generating the definition statement for the design—is critical. We know when we ask students to choose among limitless options that they can have a difficult time making a decision about where to concentrate. The empathy work done until this point may have surfaced many characteristics and qualities about the design partner. Now we ask designers to use their empathy insights to "narrow their focus" by processing the empathy chart and the insights derived from it. This is similar to the chart you filled out as part of your empathy exercise with a student you completed earlier in this chapter.

The Three-Column Chart

A three-column chart helps generate a slightly different perspective than the empathy chart, and it will help to document some of the many inferences and insights that are being culled from the empathy work. We set up this chart with a column of words that describe the design partner, a column on

Four Stages of Design Thinking Process

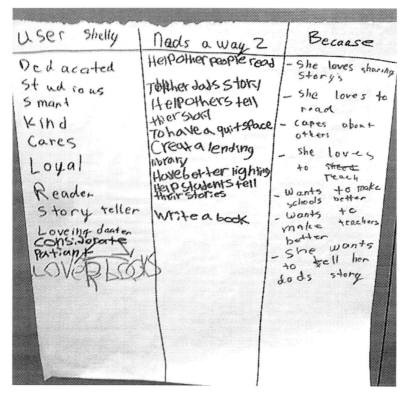

Figure 2.5 Three-column chart from a group of student designers processing interview data
(Credit: Shelley Goldman)

what needs of the partner were identified, and a "Because" column where the design thinker can speculate about the end goals, issues, or problems of their design partner. The picture (Figure 2.5) shows how a group of student designers set up their three-column chart after an interview they did with Shelley during a challenge to design spaces for stories.

Ask the following questions to start filling out the three-column empathy chart:

- Who did you meet? Describe your user.
- What was the most surprising story you heard?
- What did he/she care about the most? What frustrates him/her?
- What is he/she hoping for? What are their goals?

Empathizing

Once the three-column chart is completed, you have all the necessary prerequisites needed for crafting a PoV statement.

Defining a Solution Space and a Point of View Based on Empathy Work

The PoV statement is the last step in the empathy process. The PoV statement is the statement that will focus the direction that your solutions will take. If you look at the examples of the charts that we've provided in Figure 2.4 and Figure 2.5, you can see that many descriptions and insights about the design partner have been revealed. Figure 2.6 is an example of an empathy and three-column chart that a group created about another educator.

The Point of View Statement

The final step on the empathy stage is to define the focus of the solution space for which you will design. This is a time and part of the staging that requires making choices. While you have probably surfaced descriptions of

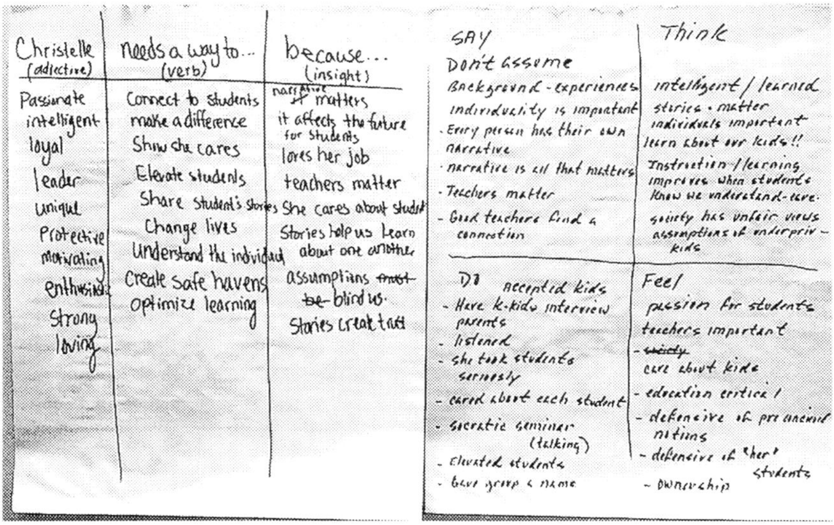

Figure 2.6 An empathy map alongside a three-column chart
(Credit: Shelley Goldman)

Four Stages of Design Thinking Process

Point of View Statement

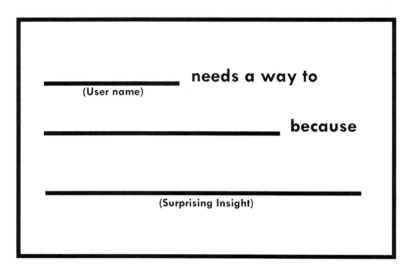

Figure 2.7 Template for writing Point of View (PoV) statements
(Credit: Saya Iwasaki)

your design partner and have made some inferences, this is the time for you to define what you will focus on. We define a direction and mandate for the rest of the design thinking project as the last act on the empathy stage.

We recommend using a simple template for all PoV statements. This way, you can always write definition statements and have your students learn to write them. The empathy chart and the three-column chart are immensely helpful for crafting the PoV statement for the design solution and it corresponds with the three columns of the chart. If you create some linkages between items in each column of the chart, you can experiment with making several possible definition statements based on the links. Once you have a few combinations of descriptions about your design partner, their needs, and end goals, the PoV statement can be chosen.

Figure 2.7 shows the template for a defining statement that captures your partner's needs:

Checking the PoV Statement

The PoV statement will become the blueprint for your design thinking solutions, so you will want to make sure it is constructed in ways that will help advance your work rather than limit it. When you choose the adjectives to describe your design partner, make sure to choose those you think are most central and important. For example, from the charts in Figure 2.6 above, we might choose the following descriptions of Christelle: "passionate, protective, leader Christelle". Those descriptors were chosen because they paired well with the one need that would be central, "to share stories of students". Note that only one need was chosen around which to design. Also notice that this *needs* section of the statement started with an **action of the partner** and we start the phrase with as a verb. It is an action statement. A statement of a solution is avoided at this point, including a solution in the PoV statement which could limit the ultimate solution set. The PoV statement should be open to many solution possibilities. And last, the statement is completed by including some goal, issue, want, or need of your partner that was uncovered during the empathy work and then recorded in the three-column chart. This last part of the template may reveal the insecurities, emotions, or aspirations of your partner that seemed to be lingering on or below the surface.

Here is an example of a basic and a more elaborated example of a PoV statement:

> The *basic version* of a PoV statement:
> *A busy mom needs a way to lower her utility bills because she wants to start conserving.*
>
> Here is an example of an *elaborated PoV statement*:
> *Olivia, a dedicated mother of four, who worries about the world her children and grandchildren will grow up in, needs a way to seamlessly integrate awareness of both waste and conservation in her daily routines because she feels shame when other moms talk about their contributions to the environment.*

You can see that the elaborated statement gives us much more insight into Olivia. It also opens up the design solution space by not being so specific to talk about simply "read her utility bills", but expanding to "seamlessly integrate awareness". This gives the design team a lot more space for design possibilities.

Four Stages of Design Thinking Process

Once you or your students have written a PoV statement, you can evaluate it to make sure it will work for the next stages in the design thinking process.

- Does the statement have any solutions written into it? If yes, keep working at it. For example, you would not want the statement to say, "Mom Olivia needs a video to show her how to track her energy use from month to month". That would be the solution to the problem and would limit other solutions.
- Next check for deep descriptions. The basic statement does not tell us what motivates Olivia, while the elaborated one does. This is important because you can then make sure that solutions fit the design partner's feelings, mandates, and goals. Make sure the statement recognizes the humanness and uniqueness of your design partner.
- Make sure the needs part of the statement is action oriented and is about what your design partner will do.

With a PoV statement developed and checked, you are ready to step off the empathy stage and onto the brainstorming stage. You now have a focus for your design that incorporates the PoV of the design partner.

You have narrowed your focus to one of many you might have chosen for your design partner, so you are ready to start working on solutions. You now have taken the steps in the empathy process. You have:

- Prepared for, engaged in, and taken notes in conjunction with an empathy gathering activity with a design partner
- Reflected using questions and tools such as empathy charts, three-column charts, and crafting a PoV statement.

We advise that all of this effort will pay off in the next stages of the design process and make the next stages of the work responsive to the needs of the design partner and other end users of the design.

We suggest that you and your students save empathy charts and notes from the empathy stage. You might return to them again and again as you work through the next stages of the process. Congratulations on learning to base your design thinking projects in empathy. We prepare to leave the empathy stage and move to the brainstorming one, with just a few summary words about why exercising empathy for us and our students is worthwhile.

Final Words on Empathy

Not too long ago, during a presentation about design thinking work we were making to a local school board, a school board member asked about why we emphasize empathy at the center of our strategic work with teachers to improve services to students designated as English learners. They asked, "Aren't teachers already incredibly empathetic people"? We answered that they are indeed empathetic, and if we gave them an empathy survey, they would all score at the top of the empathy charts, showing it as a trait they possessed. The response continued. We noted that being highly empathetic does not mean that you constantly bring it to the fore in problem-solving or that you know how to act on it. We all need to learn how to build upon our inclinations to be naturally empathetic in order to gain insights based on empathy and turn them into actions on behalf of our students. As educators, we can be generally empathetic, but we may be unable to exercise our empathy in what we do with our students due to the pressures and the influences of daily school demands. It takes work. The empathy process can help us devise ways to see our students from new focal points and with new perspectives, and that this is essential when we are trying to find new solutions to inequalities and better ways to meet students' needs. When we integrate empathy work in our teaching or with our students in their learning and integrate it into designing solutions to complex problems, we act humanely and with eyes wide open. That can only be a plus.

References

Alexander, J. J., & Sandahl, I. (2016). *The Danish way of parenting: What the happiest people in the world know about raising confident, capable kids*. Penguin.

Davidson, R. J., & Begley, S. (2013). *The emotional life of your brain: How its unique patterns affect the way you think, feel, and live—and how you can change them*. Penguin.

Lieberman, M. D. (2013). *Social: Why our brains are wired to connect.* Oxford: Oxford University Press.

Stanford d.school. https://dschool.stanford.edu/

Singer, T., Seymour, B., O'doherty, J., Kaube, H., Dolan, R. J., & Frith, C. D. (2004). Empathy for pain involves the affective but not sensory components of pain. *Science, 303*(5661), 1157–1162.

3 Brainstorming

Figure 3.1
(Credit: Saya Iwasaki)

Molly stood with one of the design teams during the Utah Shelter Challenge. The team had been assigned to work specifically on animal shelters and had interviewed someone who had recently adopted a pet from a local shelter in Salt Lake City. The woman, who had young children, had ruminated on the challenges of connecting with a pet in the loud, overwhelming, impersonal environment of the animal shelter. The team decided that she needed a way for her family to experience the different potential forever puppies in an environment that felt more like home. This was the intention that they brought onto the next stage of the design process—brainstorming.

We taught the team the rules for brainstorming. We gave each member of the team sticky notes and a marker. We asked them to stand in their design space. We played some high-energy music and set a visible timer to 10 minutes for all teams to see. We told them we

Four Stages of Design Thinking Process

want as many ideas as they could imagine. We shared a few rules of brainstorming and said "Go!"

Brainstorming can sometimes be a reluctant and exhilarating process. There is tension as individuals sort out who will volunteer a design idea first and who will add to ideas. There can be a moment of silence as the team members formulate their first idea, but once the first sticky note hits the chart paper, it opens the space for others to contribute.

On this day in Utah, the adults on the team made space for a student to share first. A middle school girl said, "There should be a couch". She was picking up on an idea from the user interview when the woman who adopted the dog explained that once she was home with adopted dog after a few hours, it had curled up in her daughter's lap on the couch and they had breathed a collective sigh of relief because the family had finally connected with their new fur baby.

Remembering the same portion of this interview, the elementary teacher in the group said, "Yes, and there needs to be more time". As she spoke, she wrote "more time" on a sticky note and placed it on the chart paper next to the sticky note that said "COUCH". From here, the flood gates opened and each team member took turns writing a sticky note, sharing it aloud, and placing it into the design space.

Eight minutes into the session, the natural flow of ideas started to slow down. The design team began looking around the room to see if others were still going strong. As their coach, Molly stepped in and asked them how they might design the shelter experience if they were the animals being adopted. She asked them to take a moment to picture what they learned in the interview about how the dogs in the shelter were feeling. What did these animals need to show themselves during the adoption process? This led the team to a new burst of ideas captured on colored sticky notes and poured onto the wall. At this time, this team had more than 80 sticky notes capturing ideas to meet their design partner's needs.

What Is Brainstorming?

To brainstorm is to generate ideas. In design thinking, **brainstorming** is a creative activity where a team of people work together to list ideas that respond to a specific prompt. In the case of design thinking, teams are typically brainstorming in response to a need within a problem space that they have identified. In some circles, this is referred to as ideating—the act of generating ideas.

During background building and empathy, design facilitators are often reminding folks that it is not yet time for solutions. This sometimes frustrates people, especially those who consider themselves as problem-solvers in their families and workspaces. Once the brainstorming stage lights go on, it is time to generate all kinds of solutions. The act of team brainstorming has something for everyone. For those who are right-brained, who see a problem and want to jump right to solving it, brainstorming is the part of the process where you finally get to contribute solution ideas. The right brain craves logic and solutions, and this is where design team members get to flex those muscles. For those who are left-brained, who relished in the empathy and ambiguity of the previous parts of the process, brainstorming is a chance to channel the big emotions solicited from interviews into creative solutions that would make the world better for their user. In brainstorming, we encourage teams to capture ideas in pictures as well as words and this is another outlet for the non-linear thinkers on design teams.

With students it is also true that brainstorming is a place where everyone can contribute. If you set the stage correctly (and we will tell you just how to do this in the next section), the act of brainstorming is one where all voices can be heard.

For example, in a workshop where student design teams were generating solutions related to re-integrating veterans into society, a 6th-grade girl named Natalia began participating verbally during the brainstorming phase of the challenge. This was an intensive 2-day challenge and Natalia had been attentive but silent during the entire first day. When we spoke with the teachers from her school, they explained that she was an English language learner and that she was not comfortable speaking in English. Knowing this, we were tentative and gentle in prompting her to share an idea with her team. Finally during the brainstorming phase, Natalia's voice rose inside of her as she shared the opening idea. It was quick but she had heard that every idea was welcome and knew this was a safe space to enter the conversation. Her entry into the process emboldened her to continue sharing ideas during the rest of the challenge.

Four Stages of Design Thinking Process

 Stages of Brainstorming

The brainstorming phase of a design challenge has three stages.

- First, you must teach your design teams how to brainstorm. For seasoned design thinkers, this may be simply reviewing the rules as a set of agreements. Even students and designers who have been through several challenges benefit from a reorientation to the rules.
- The second stage of brainstorming is action oriented and consists of activities to generate and share ideas.
- The third stage of brainstorming is idea selection. This is the part of the process where teams move from their enormous list of ideas to the one or two ideas that they decide to prioritize and ultimately take forward in the process.

The subsequent sections describe the conditions and nuances for each of these stages of brainstorming.

Stage 1: Introducing the Rules for Brainstorming

How do we create the space for design teams to brainstorm effectively? We teach a set of rules for brainstorming. These are useful whether your students are brainstorming during a design challenge or brainstorming as part of another classroom activity. They are also helpful for faculty brainstorming activities.

#1 Open Minds and Open Hearts

This is the quintessential brainstorming rule and the one that created the space for Natalia and many others like her to participate in this process. The open minds and open hearts rule for brainstorming asks designers to restrict judgement of themselves and others. When you restrict judgment, you do not judge any idea that comes to mind. If it pops into your head, you share it with the group. If you think it is mundane or stupid or similar or far-fetched, you share it, no matter what. Being radically open to what pops into your mind is your first responsibility to the group. For this to be successful, team members must agree to have open minds. The second responsibility of the group is to proceed with an "open heart" or to restrict judgement on any idea shared by another team member. If you think some else's idea is mundane or stupid or similar or far-fetched, you accept it without verbal or physical commentary.

#2 Share the Headline

In design thinking, as in life, many ideas pop into our heads with vivid detail and intense hedging (statements that start with "that would work, but only if…") and other complex modifiers. There will be room for all of this evaluation and modification of an idea in the prototyping phase. During brainstorming, it is essential that team members do not indulge in sharing these details. This is called headlining because you are asking designers to share only the headline of their story. If you are going to get 100 ideas on to the board in 10 minutes, there is only room for the headline that captures the essence of each idea.

In the introduction to this chapter, the student might have explained the details of why a couch was important, of what she heard that made her think this, and advocate for what a couch in an animal shelter would accomplish but instead she simply said "COUCH". The amazing thing about the design process was that her teammates were on a shared journey with her and many of the details underlying her suggestion were invoked for the group as she uttered a single syllable.

#3 One Mic

As we write for an audience of teachers, the **One Mic** as a rule seems almost too obvious to expand on. While this is true, we find brainstorming rules to be an exceptional opportunity to provide explicit instructions to students about this rule as it comes with an authentic opportunity to practice. For those who haven't heard this phrase, **One Mic** is the rule that only one person talks at a time. When teaching the rules for brainstorming, it is fun to do a skit where students are asked to break particular rules and then have the class analyze what went wrong. It is very clear to students, when observing from the outside, that when everyone talks at once or someone is constantly interrupting or dominating the conversation, it undermines the spirit of the exercise. The goal for brainstorming is to gather infinite solutions to complex problems and when team members do not give others the chance to share their headline, the end result is weakened by repeated ideas and hurt feelings. To avoid this, during our workshops, we encourage participants of all ages to keep an ear on the group as each individual writes/sketches their next idea on a sticky note. When there is a pause in sharing, the one with the ideas speaks the headline, sticks the note on the wall, and listens for the next idea.

#4 Yes and…

Yes and… means to build on the ideas of others. As humans we have the tendency to vet ideas on arrival. You hear a new idea and the tendency is to say **Yes but…** and state the reasons why the solution won't work as well as the one the listener feels more invested in. In this sense, the **Yes and…** rule is related to "Open Mind and Open Heart" as the essence of both is to limit the urge to judge ourselves and others. The "Yes and…" rule builds upon "Open Mind and Open Heart" because it also gives designers a frame with which to build upon the ideas of one another.

When teaching this rule, we ask our teams to sit in a circle and plan a party (you give any challenge here but if you are drawing a blank, this one never fails to get a group going). We ask groups to nominate someone in each group to count ideas for party planning over two rounds. In the first round, participants are only allowed to respond to one another by starting their sentence with **Yes but…** followed by whatever comes to mind next. What tends to result when a sentence starts with **Yes but…** is a criticism, or a competing idea.

In the second round, participants are only allowed to respond to one another saying **Yes and…** followed by a comment. When we debrief, we get the tally for each round and not surprisingly, the **Yes and…** round produces a greater number of ideas than the **Yes but…** round by at least 200%. We also ask individuals to share how they feel during each round. In the **Yes but…** round, they feel judged, anxious, and eventually closed down. This is true even when they know others have been directed to be critical in this way. **Yes but…** closes the valve of creativity in its tracks. During the **Yes and…** round we hear students and adults alike descend into uproarious laughter. They report creative juices flowing and unexpected turns of creativity.

As is the case in this introductory activity, the premise of the **Yes and…** rule is to ask design teams to catch and correct themselves and their teammates if one should utter a "BUT". The flip side of this rule is that **Yes and...** can be used to build upon existing ideas when an individual feels like they are running low on new ideas. In research that Shelley and the REDlab team completed, the team found that the team members using **Yes and...** formulations throughout the design activities had also had the most uptake on their design suggestions (Goldman et al. 2014). We recommend that students listen closely to the ideas of their teammates and as soon as possible, utter **Yes and...** then allow their brain to fill in the blank with an addition or variation of the existing suggestion.

#5 Never Enough

The **Never Enough** rule is intended to promote the highest possible quantity of ideas during a given brainstorming session. It is commonly the case that the most creative ideas come after a team feels like they are done or that they have shared every possible idea they can collectively summon. The truth is that not all innovation is obvious, and it is important that design thinkers dig deep during brainstorming. Sometimes, as facilitators, you can offer numerical quantities (100 ideas in 10 minutes). When we do this in our workshops or lessons, we ask teams who meet the original goal to give us 20 more before sitting down.

It is not necessary to give a numerical quantity. Alternatively, a design facilitator can monitor the teams to identify when a team has hit a lull. The job of the facilitator (which you play as teacher) in these moments is to act as the unflappable cheerleader for the team. No matter what they throw at you, explain that you believe that they can give you another 20, 40, 60 ideas before time is out. Silence and waiting has no place in brainstorming. If teams seem stuck, you can also give them a prompt to help them refocus (see Mindful Facilitation techniques in section "Mindful Facilitation in Brainstorming Stage 2" for details on these prompts). Remind them that in a brainstorm no idea is a bad idea.

There are many variations to the rules for brainstorming found online. Many are variations of the rules listed here. Others that you may want to bring forward with your students or colleagues include sharing in pictures and words, nominating a designated scribe, staying on topic, and finding ways to shift perspectives. We use some of these variations depending on the group and goals for brainstorming and encourage you to make a list that feels right for your use case.

Stage 2: The Act of Brainstorming

In addition to teaching the rules for brainstorming, it is also important to set the stage for brainstorming in a few particular ways. As someone leading a group into brainstorming, it is important to consider space, color, movement, music, time, and mindful facilitation.

Space

First, provide ample space for teams to brainstorm. Imagine team members with sticky notes and a large piece of chart paper to collect all of their suggestions. Other options include butcher paper, large whiteboards, and online brainstorming apps. (Pro-tip: the reason we prefer sticky notes to whiteboards is that sticky notes allow teams to interact with their ideas after the fact. Sticky notes are tactile and easy to move around and cluster by categories, and that can help teams parse the landscape of solutions in front of them.)

Color

In a brainstorming space, it is helpful for participants to have options for colors. This can be accomplished by providing different colors of marker, sticky notes, or both. A colorful space stimulates creativity and provides visual variation in the landscape of solutions. It also helps people keep track of different ideas. If you are staring at a sea of blue stickies, it can be hard to find the one you are referencing in later conversation. Conversely, if you know that all of Natalia's ideas were on pink paper, you can scan for the one you are looking for and fold it into conversation more quickly.

Movement

While setting the stage for brainstorming, it is also essential to create an environment where teams can be standing. The first thing we do before a workshop is to create individual wall spaces where teams will work for the duration of the challenge. If we run out of wall spaces, we sometimes stand a long table or desk on its small side so it positions as a vertical wall space. For all phases of design thinking, but especially for brainstorming, standing is essential to the creative process. Research indicates that physical movement increases creativity. In one study from the Stanford Graduate

School of Education (GSE), participants were asked to generate potential uses for an everyday object while standing and walking while others executed this task seated at a desk across from the researcher. Those in the movement category offered a significantly higher quantity of responses and demonstrated higher levels of creativity than those who were seated (see Oppezzo & Schwartz 2014 or Reynolds 2014). As a facilitator of design, it is likely that you will encounter students and colleagues who will push back on this and groan at your insistence that designers stand. In these moments, you will find that the reward for fearless cheerleading to promote standing leads to increased creativity and engagement.

Music

Another element that can be used to set the stage for brainstorming is music. Play upbeat music that enourages teams to wiggle a little as they complete the task. We recommend something that makes people tap their toes and get their blood flowing (e.g., "Can't Stop the Feeling" by Justin Timberlake or "Happy" by Pharrell Williams). Once you are brainstorming regularly, your students might help you create a brainstorming playlist.

Time

The next consideration when planning a brainstorming exercise is time. Often, novice designers want to luxuriate in generating solutions but when given too much time, design teams start to break the headline rule or drift off task. When determining time for brainstorming, it is important to convey a sense of urgency. For a full-day feature challenge, we often start with 10 minutes for the part of brainstorming activities where ideas are generated and shared. Then we read the room and usually offer an additional 5 minutes to encourage the teams and emphasize the need for a high quantity of ideas. Always start by announcing less time than you think they will need but provisioning for slightly more in your agenda.

Mindful Facilitation in Brainstorming Stage 2

If you notice a team is getting stuck during a brainstorming session, there are a few tools you can use to re-engage a team. This section describes three facilitation techniques to guide struggling teams.

Changing the Frame

The first thing you can try to get a team unstuck is to introduce a new frame for the brainstorm. You can do this by asking team members to change it up and think about the challenge very differently than the current track they are on. Examples of this include: "how would you solve this…

- If you were an alien from outer space?
- If you were a 4-year-old boy?
- If you were 50 years in the future"?

You can also change the frame by asking teams to eliminate perceived constraints. If you notice a team is getting caught up in "Yes buts" or is stagnating in the face of the improbability of executing their ideas, you can ask them questions that help them work around the perceived limitation. Examples of this include: "how would you solve this…

- If you had a team of 100 to work on it?
- A 5-million-dollar budget?
- If you had unlimited space?
- If you had 10 years to perfect before launching"?

Reconnecting with the Purpose

Another mindful facilitation tool is to remind the teams of their point of view (PoV) statement. When a team is stuck, it often helps to return to the user's PoV and use it as a north star to guide brainstorming. You might stand with a team and read the statement aloud slowly or have a student read it aloud with feeling to see if circling back to this document stimulates new responses.

Asking "How Might We… "? Questions

Alternatively, you can try reframing the PoV statement as a "How might we… "? question. In the example from the start of this chapter, we may have posed the challenge as:

> How might we create an adoption experience that allows potential pet owners to make lasting connections with available dogs?

When posing a "How might we…"?, it is helpful to record it at the top of a piece of chart paper. If time permits, have the team list one or two or ten additional "How might we…?" questions that are inspired by their empathy maps and PoV statements.

The "How might we…?" can serve as a bridge between a need and a solution in a form that is more concrete than generating solutions in response to PoV statements. This is because having the PoV reframed in question form invites the brain to answer the question. Additionally, if you have multiple "How might we…"? questions, slight variations in wording and focus can lead to wildly different responses in brainstorming. That said, when time permits, drafting "How might we…"? questions can be an excellent scaffold for brainstorming.

As you experiment with controlling these elements in a way that makes sense in your space for your students or colleagues, you can use this list as a tool for reflection or a guide for bringing your facilitation technique to the next level. If a brainstorming session felt coerced or was not particularly fruitful, how might you modify one or more of these elements in future sessions to maximize creativity and output? As facilitators of design thinking, you can almost always modify space, color, movement, music, time, and facilitation techniques to help teams find their flow.

Stage 3: The Process for Selecting Ideas

More often than not, it is appropriate to end a brainstorming session by scaffolding the process of idea selection. When brainstorming is facilitated well, it is a highly generative high-energy activity that leaves design thinkers with a rush of endorphins. They have finally been allowed to start solving the problem and been dropped into a set of circumstances that allows them to do this with more perspective and less constraint than is typical when solving problems in daily life. As facilitator, you have just opened the door for a sea of uncensored ideas, and it is essential that you provide brainstorming teams with as much scaffolding for narrowing these ideas down as you did for getting them to generate the ideas.

At a recent training for school and district leadership from an under-resourced district outside of Chicago, a participant remarked how he appreciated the way the process had opened the space for his team to solve problems in radically different ways than they had ever imagined. He called it "unbound creativity" and explained how different this felt from the usual constraint-based methods they typically employed for solving problems at the district office. His team had participated in a 6-month challenge with a focus on graduation rates. In an early homework assignment for the design thinking course, the team had identified users as non-traditional students defined in terms of credit deficiency. After a series of student interviews, they expanded their definition of non-traditional students to include other archetypes, such as those students with strong intellectual capacity who also navinavigate significant challenges outside of school.

After completing several empathy maps, the district office team drafted a PoV statement, "Non-traditional students need a way to understand the myriad of resources available for their lives during and after school because productive citizenship depends on planning for and taking steps to cultivate the life you want after high school". They used this as a frame for brainstorming and filled countless sticky notes with potential solutions to meet this need.

At our final meeting, the team presented a new program within the district that would focus on meeting the needs of non-traditional students. The team was awaiting board approval on funding for a pilot in the coming year where they would house a flexible academic program featuring credit recovery, work internships, accelerated graduation options, and counseling for students choosing to re-enter their assigned traditional school. They had identified a location, drafted a budget, and forged community partnerships as they prepared to test a subset of the solutions that emerged from a single brainstorming session conducted earlier that year.

How did this team go from a sea of sticky notes to a set of actionable ideas to move forward? How does any team do this work? Idea selection is tricky because when it is not facilitated well, teams can face a dramatic drop from the exhilarating high of unfettered brainstorming to a situation where team members are deadlocked while campaigning for one idea over another. In the case of the district office, after the idea generation session, the teams were asked to cluster their sticky notes so that similar ideas were arranged together. Next, they were introduced to a voting protocol to help them narrow the ideas in their landscape. Each team member was given one vote to assign to an idea in each category.

Figure 3.2 was presented as voting protocol was presented and team members voted.

Using the symbols from Figure 3.2 and the process described in the text box, the non-traditional student team narrowed their thinking down to

Brainstorming

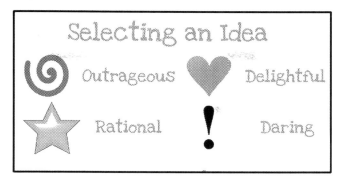

Figure 3.2 Prompt for voting by assigning symbols exercise
(Credit: Molly B. Zielezinski)

Voting by Assigning Symbols

- The swirl is awarded for an idea that is outrageous and impractical but your favorite nevertheless.
- The heart is awarded to that one sweetheart idea that makes you swoon to think about as a possible outcome.
- The star is awarded for the idea that is you think is both rational and doable.
- The exclamation point is awarded for those ideas that are "out there", but for some reason, you just can't give them up.

After the team sorts their ideas and cast votes, a subset of ideas begins to gain emphasis based on the number of votes received. This happens when you have a lot of ideas of a similar type or when you have a number of votes centered around a particular idea or group of ideas.

three major ideas: flexible schedule, career pipelines, and accelerated curriculum pathways. Each was represented within their final prototype and pitch to the board.

Classification and Evaluation

The methods offered to the design teams in this challenge were not unique. The scaffolding consisted of two different critical thinking tasks—classification and evaluation. While our story featured adults, you can and should support student designers in the same ways. The classification component of idea selection involves making judgments about how different solutions interrelate and what features of each solution distinguish it as aligned with one theme over another. To facilitate teams to this end, ask them to sort the results of their brainstorming into categories. It is not uncommon for one or more groups to begin this process without even being prompted and when this happens, it is a good practice to use these design teams as a positive example of how to move forward with idea selection.

Once ideas are classified, encourage individuals to evaluate ideas given a predetermined set of criteria. The evaluation portion of idea selection, in the case of the district office team, was executed through the voting protocol detailed above. These categories are a great starting point for a facilitator, but they can be customized to support a nuanced learning objective as needed. For example, for younger students, it can helpful to limit the prompt to voting to more accessible categories such as:

- favorite idea
- most fun
- easiest
- most innovative
- most helpful

Alternatively, you can incorporate more sophisticated category types that align with learning objectives. For example, if students have brainstormed constructive next steps for Juliet at a particular moment within Shakespeare's classic text, you might ask students to vote for:

- the most socially appropriate action given the historical context
- the most emotionally validating action
- the most ethical action
- the best action if Juliet were alive today

Another way to sort and classify is to rank responses in relation to a new set of constraints. For example, if students have brainstormed elements they might include in a research station for Antarctic scientists, after brainstorming, you might introduce new constraints related to budget or materials. In cases like this, you can have students order the appropriateness of solutions in response to the newly identified constraints. In another example, if students are brainstorming class pets, you may ask them to cast a vote in favor of the animal that would bring them the most joy and a vote against the animal that has the most potential to disrupt the learning community. In this example, the constraint might be noise or smell.

In each of these cases—the more general and the more nuanced criteria for evaluating ideas—it is excellent practice to ask team members to give their rationale for voting the way that they did. For example, one student might say they voted against dogs as a classroom pet because several classmates are allergic. Another student might say they voted against a bird because they are noisy in a way that can be distracting during class time. Sharing rationale for one's judgments in this way elevates the critical thinking task from simply evaluating ideas to evaluating ideas and justifying your thinking. Providing novice design thinkers with this kind of authentic opportunity to engage in dialogue that encourages them to both justify their thinking and engage critically with the perspective of others on their team is both useful as a learning opportunity and helpful in advancing the idea selection process.

When Teams Can't Find Common Ground

Occasionally, after classifying ideas, evaluating ideas, justifying thinking, and perspective-taking within the group, you will find a team that remains staunchly divided. If time and resources allow, you may encourage teams like this to divide and conquer. The team can split into equal groups to build out two totally different prototypes, possibly recombining once they have collected feedback from users later on. This type of split is common in the tech industry as technology designers build out two different user experiences and compare them via A/B testing. Advancing multiple viable paths forward can be challenging but is a great mirror for real life. Also, it is quite common that once given permission and encouragement to pursue two totally different ideas, inflexible team members begin to soften to the ideas of others allowing the team to converge around a single path forward. Alternatively, split teams may find a way to combine their ideas into a single prototype moving forward. No matter the resolution, while navigating the disagreement, team members have been given an authentic opportunity to exercise real-world critical thinking skills.

References

Goldman, S., Kabayadondo, Z., Royalty, A., Carroll, M. P., & Roth, B. (2014). Student Teams in Search of Design Thinking. In *Design thinking research* (pp. 11–34). Cham: Springer.

Oppezzo, M., & Schwartz, D. L. (2014). Give your ideas some legs: The positive effect of walking on creative thinking. *Journal of experimental psychology: learning, memory, and cognition*, *40*(4), 1142.

Reynolds, G. Want to be more Creative? Take a walk. *New York Times*. April 30, 2014. ps://well.blogs.nytimes.com/2014/04/30/want-to-be-more-creative-take-a-walk/

 # Prototyping Cycles

Figure 4.1
(Credit: Saya Iwasaki)

After 1.5 days of design thinking bootcamp, the first Utah shelter team was ready to present their prototype to their design partner for feedback. Rather than handing her an object or a model of a shiny new animal shelter, this team chose to share their thinking using an "experience prototype". They carved out a section of the cafeteria where we were working and arranged the furniture into multiple rooms. The room they spent the most time on was called the "Living Room". The "Living Room" had a bed, a couch, dog toys, and a door to an outside space.

The design team had organized school furniture the best they could in order to convey the look and feel of a traditional living room. They added labels where necessary and built some elements out of design materials (such as dog toys out of pipe cleaners). When their design partner arrived for the feedback session, they treated her as if she had arrived at a dog shelter and explained the process as if they were shelter employees. After selecting a dog from photos that she would like to get to know better, they brought her

DOI: 10.4324/9780429273421-5

into the "Living Room" explaining that she could spend as much time as she liked in here with this dog or any other. She asked if she could bring her family back later and they warmly encouraged her to do so. They left her alone in the room with the make-believe dog and she used the features they had built to fill a bowl of water for him before sitting down to play. At this moment, the designers popped into the "Living Room" and explained that if she would like to interact with the dog off leash outside, she could come through the door to the "Back Yard" but that beyond the fence, she could take him around the block on the leash with the supervision of an employee.

After the design partner spent 15 minutes engaging with the design team actors and exploring the features of the prototype, the team switched gears. They asked her about questions she had and how she felt this shelter might work in real life after spending time in the "experience prototype". They asked her what she liked and what she might change. They also asked her how this experience compared to her recent dog adoption experience. One team member led this interview while the others took notes and chimed in with clarifying questions. The feedback from their design partner was both direct and actionable. By providing a "home-like" environment to get to know the potential pet, they had radically and necessarily improved on elements of the adoption experience. But there were some aspects that she thought needed improvement. She mentioned a need to understand how a pet would respond to a family meal or being left at the front door when the family left for school and work in the morning.

After the design partner left, the team discussed the feedback, then began updating and revising based on it. In doing this, they worked together to complete one full prototyping cycle. A prototyping cycle begins as design teams move from idea selection to the creation of a tangible item/experience in the world. From there, designers get feedback on their creation and make changes based on this feedback. This, like other stages in the design process, can loop back on itself almost infinitely, but in a two-day workshop, we typically call it done after one round of revisions.

What Is a Prototyping Cycle?

A prototyping cycle is the part of the design thinking process where designers bring potential solutions to life. In design thinking, it is important to begin the first prototyping cycle with a low-resolution prototype, or quick mockups that are intended to get an idea across to a potential end-user of the design. The low-resolution prototypes are put in front of design partners as prompts or stimuli for gathering feedback. When a team improves a prototype based on feedback, it is called iterating. The more iterations a team goes through in the design thinking process, the better the eventual solution. As design teams progress from their first prototype through subsequent iterations, the quality and detail of a prototype improves incrementally. In workshops with adults or when solving real-world problems, it is common to be asked "How will I know when my design is done"? The answer is that you are done designing when you've reached your deadline. Without a deadline for finishing a project, the prototype and iteration cycle could continue infinitely as designers tinker towards an unachievable "perfect" solution. Thus, it is essential to keep project and curriculum deadlines in mind and create a scope and sequence that affords design teams time for one or more iterations based on design partner feedback. You must draw a line and limit additional time beyond the cycles you plan.

Why Should You Start with a Low-Resolution Prototype?

Low-resolution prototypes are Design Thinking 101, especially for K-12 challenges. Imagine what a mistake it would be if a design team invested substantial time and effort into developing a high-resolution prototype. They have spent a lot of time and resources on the prototype. They have also become highly invested in the prototype's success. Then, when they find out that their prototype does not meet their design partner's needs, they suffer major setbacks. They may have lost a lot of time. If the prototype is of a real-world product that would have gone to market, they may have lost a lot of money. They may also have misinterpreted or ignored the human-centered imperative of design thinking. If instead, design teams start rough and build towards higher resolution in response to the feedback of design partners and end users, they are able to calibrate with thoughts, feelings, and values and be agile and responsive. This opens the door for a responsive innovation that stretches well beyond what a single team member values.

What Supplies Do You Need for Prototyping?

There is no set supply list required for prototyping. Very early prototypes can be sketches completed with paper and pencil. Designers can even

Four Stages of Design Thinking Process

engage in low-resolution app design with some printouts of storyboards or wireframes (i.e., outline of a phone screen or browser with open space for the designer to fill in a sketch).

For hands-on design, we recommend a random assortment of the items listed below. We often give this list with the following caveat: *this is a wish list. It is not necessary to have every item on this list and alternatives are welcome.* In classrooms, we highly recommend that students begin to bring in recyclable materials from home a week or more in advance of prototyping. We also recommend that teachers embarking on a design challenge send an email to school staff requesting bizarre, exciting, or mundane additions that can be contributed to the materials set. Even the mundane can be repurposed during the prototyping phase. For example, one 5th-grade boy fashioned a model of a shag carpet out of staples while creating a welcoming 3-D model welcome center for veterans transitioning from military service to home. In another example seen in Figure 4.2, a team of teachers used egg cartons to imagine individual study carousels in a 21st-century media center prototype. This team was responding to a need for silent study spaces that surfaced during interviews with students.

Figure 4.2 Prototype example showing use of egg cartons to depict study carousels for a media center redesign project
(Credit: Molly B. Zielezinski)

Prototyping Cycles

Prototyping Wishlist
Building

- Lots of cardboard
  - packing boxes
  - cereal boxes
  - toilet paper rolls
- Egg cartons
- Bubble wrap or other packing materials
- Paperclips
- Pipe cleaners
- Rubber bands
- Yarn, string, thread
- Lunch bags
- Plastic bags
- Butcher paper
- Old magazines, books, or brochures
- Grocery bags, plastic, or paper
- Popsicle sticks
- straws
- Foam, clay, or playdough
- Fabric scraps
- Wood scraps

Adhesives

- Staplers
- Glue
- Painter's tape
- Masking tape
- Scotch tape
- Rubber cement
- Glue sticks

Tools

- X-Acto knives and/or
- Box cutters
- Scissors for each team
- Staplers and staples
- Glue guns

Inspirational Extras

- Feathers
- Poof balls
- Googly eyes
- Beans or beads
- Found objects of interest/materials that represent student culture or background (e.g., student photos, old art projects, etc.).

Some schools are fortunate to have a dedicated space that is well-stocked for design. Often this is a fabrication lab that includes high-end machines such as 3D printers, laser cutters, and power tools. With access to a fab lab comes temptation to skip the low-resolution prototype. If students can make working models cut perfectly out of wood, why wouldn't they? The reason for this is that these machines can take a lot of time, working experience, and ability to handle frustration to operate. Students lose time learning to make their precise vision a reality and this happens at the expense of time for feedback and iteration with lower resolution prototypes. Often, by the time students have created some vision of their sketch with power tools, they have missed the opportunity to improve their design based on feedback.

Given this, it is strongly recommended that even in these very well-resourced environments, students are still given the opportunity to bring sketches to life with cardboard and masking tape before diving into the fabrication experience. Fabrication without a low-resolution prototype is useful in engineering design projects when instructions and specs come as part of the project. In design thinking, however, it is part of the process to engage in a prototyping cycle from low resolution toward those that are of higher fidelity in order to create designs based on empathy that address unresolved human needs.

Another way to avoid the time constraints related to fabrication lab tools is to supplement design curriculum with tool-based skill builders. If these are offered outside of the design thinking process and are built regularly into the curriculum with appropriate tools introduced across the grade levels, students will have a scaffold to work upon when it is time to mobilize a power tool for a higher resolution prototype. For example, students might have to follow specific parameters to cut and assemble parts of a bird house using a lave and a drill. If they spend time during the skill builder learning to program the lave to produce certain results, they will have this experience to draw on when this tool is needed in the future. Furthermore, they will understand the types of information that is required (i.e., dimensions, material type) when they must utilize this tool to bring their own ideas, rather than a preset activity, into fruition.

Methods for Communicating Ideas as Prototypes

This chapter has alluded to several methods for communicating ideas as low-resolution prototypes. These include creating a preliminary sketch, creating a physical prototype, and creating an experience prototype. The subsequent sections provide more details about each of these methods.

Sketching Ideas

Once a design team has selected a solution, it is sometimes a good idea to have each team member take 3 minutes to sketch how they imagine this idea. This is an optional step but can be useful in helping a team synchronize around particularly abstract ideas. Sketching in advance of building can also be a way to avoid scope creep on a solution. Scope creep is unforeseen growth and expansion of a design as different team members add features that they find most valuable.

Molly remembers that during her very first design challenge, while experiencing the process as a learner for the first time, her design team was tasked with finding leisure activities for young married couples during the economic downturn. Her team, consisting of all novice design thinkers, was not very organized and ended up with a button that would turn the room into a disco and another button that would transform it into a reading nook. Without synchronizing what was most important about their multi-use community hangout space in advance, the team ended up building a nonsensical string of implausible features. In this case, a sketch in advance would have helped.

Pro-tip: when teams inevitably debate which features from sketches are to be included in the prototype, point them back to their empathy map and PoV statement. The PoV statement can be treated as a north star, shining the path forward that will allow teams to overcome egos by refocusing on their design partner and their needs.

Physical Prototypes

Physical prototypes are objects you build to convey the team's ideas about a solution. Building a physical prototype can take anywhere from 7 minutes to several class periods. One story in design lore is told often to illustrate just how simple low-resolution physical prototypes can be. In this instance, there was a designer at IDEO working with healthcare professionals to create a modern surgery tool. As the designer interviewed a surgeon, the surgeon mentioned that incision tools were unnecessarily bulky and this led to anxiety for the doctors about imprecision and also triggered watchful patients. The surgeon wished for something that fit in his hand. The designer looked around the studio and grabbed a film canister, an dry erase marker, and a snack bag clip. He taped them together and handed them to the surgeon. "Like this"? he asked. The surgeon reflected on this. He liked how it was slim and simple but explained that the marker tip was much too blunt to perform nasal surgery. The subsequent design replaced the pen cap with a long thin metal rod.

In this story, the designer used found objects to test what he imagined in response to the surgeon's need. Prototyping in this way can be the equivalent to the teacher talk move "I heard you say...did I get that right"? but instead of repeating in words, you are creating a physical solution in

Prototyping Cycles

response to an uncovered need. Low-resolution physical prototypes, like the one in this story, allow for ideas to be communicated clearly and evolve quickly.

Paper Prototypes

A paper prototype is a type of low-resolution prototype that is useful when designing content that will appear on a screen. When you are designing a technology mediated solution, it is good practice to show rather than tell a design partner what kinds of buttons and features they will encounter. In a paper prototype like this, the design team has created a sequence of screens that allows a potential user to click through a design from the home screen through subsequent screens that are essential to communicating the solution. Figure 4.3 provides a blank template for this type of work. It can be helpful to have sketches for multiple step-throughs (e.g., if the home screen has two buttons, have a sketch for what happens when you press one and another sketch for what happens if you press the other). In one example, a team of teachers learning the design process during a 2-day water conservation challenge, created a paper prototype of a GPS-informed app that allowed people to report violations such as businesses watering the sidewalk instead of the lawn or broken sprinkler heads.

Another kind of paper prototype is a storyboard. This is a set of boxes on a page with arrows illustrating the order of events. A storyboard is a useful method for prototyping when you are building a space-based solution but do not have the luxury presenting your prototype in a place where

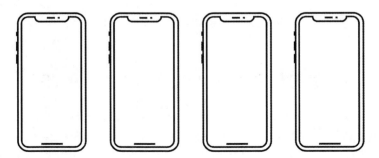

Figure 4.3 Blank template for creating a paper-based prototype of a digital experience using a mobile phone
(Credit: Saya Iwasaki)

103

you can manipulate furniture. For example, a group of students in Utah was prototyping solutions for increasing community and belonging for the Freshmen class. After stepping through empathy and brainstorming, one team decided to prototype an "Open Lunch" solution that would allow freshmen leave campus with upper class students and thereby engage in some of the fun shared experiences that they were missing. A storyboard for a solution like this can embody specific details, for example, the opening box might have a calendar with the last Friday of the month circled. Next, we would see a bell ringing, then a senior approaching their assigned freshmen. Even with simple sketches, you can bring a complex idea like this to life.

Experience Prototype

An experience prototype is an interactive skit or live experience led by a design team in a way that allows a potential end-user of the design to explore the solution. Like the example at the start of this chapter, experience prototypes are often partially scripted while also allowing the tester to engage as they would if this experience were actually happening. Experience prototypes typically involve manipulating furniture, props, and members of the design team as actors. An experience prototype is a good choice for a design team when the solution a team wishes to pose isn't a concrete object. Instead, it is a new kind of experience where the details can be communicated through an interactive skit or a run-through. Oftentimes, teams lean into physical prototypes, like scale models and dioramas when experience prototypes can be a more powerful way of illustrating to a user how this solution would feel in the world.

Gathering Feedback Using a Prototype

Once your design teams have built their prototypes, the next step is for them to gather feedback from design partners. This takes a bit of scheduling magic if you are the one facilitating the design challenge or design lessons. For example, in one school we work with, 3rd-grade students design solutions to improve the quality of daily life at school for an adult on campus. The teacher invites all the adults to the class for design team empathy interviews and each team steps through the phases of the process in subsequent lessons. When soliciting support from the local community in this way, it sometimes feels like a lot to ask for volunteers to come in for feedback rounds.

In our early workshops, we were overly sensitive to constraints on volunteer time. Rather than having those people interviewed by the teams come back, we would allow other design teams to give feedback. In time, we learned that this significantly degraded the quality of the feedback. Additionally, we found that those who were interviewed are often touched to have student and adult design teams think so deeply about them and their needs. As such, whenever possible, we recommend trying to build in follow-up interactions into the original request for volunteers.

If this is not possible, you can be somewhat flexible. For example, in another school we work with, 4th-grade students design solutions for firefighters. They take a field trip to the firehouse and each team interviews their own firefighter. In this case, it may be logistically prohibitive to get all the original participants back in touch with the students for feedback. Other options would be to have one firefighter visit the class and give feedback on behalf of their peers. Another alternative would be to have teams videoconference with their original design partner. When in doubt, get as close to the original source as possible.

Best Practices for Sharing Prototype

Before design teams gather feedback on their prototype, they must learn a few best practices that improve the quality of the feedback. First, in the moments when their design partner first encounters the prototype, design teams can feel tempted to explain everything they imagined and why. The rule of thumb here is "Show, Don't Tell". It is essential to remind design teams of this as they are getting ready for feedback, so they can add any finishing touches that will let the prototype speak for itself. When a potential design partner first steps up to a physical prototype or into an experience prototype, the design team should wait in silence as the person pokes, prods, and explores. Eventually, they will ask questions and this is when the team can intervene with its well-articulated details.

After interaction and exploration of the prototype, either as a product or an experience, it is important that the design team conducts a mini-interview with the design partner to gather feedback. You can scaffold this by asking teams to prep for their feedback by folding a paper into four quadrants and labeling each as follows:

- What works ...
- What doesn't work ...
- Questions
- Suggestions

Each quadrant is a prompt for an interview question and as in the initial interview process, digging deeper for details and stories is a useful practice in gathering feedback here as well. Teams should document all of the feedback carefully as this will be the jumping off point for iterations and improvements.

Revising Prototypes Based on Feedback

After gathering feedback, teams must go back to their prototype and prioritize what they heard. Sometimes this means gutting a whole element of their prototype and building out something totally new. Other times, teams are just polishing up a few details. Still other times, teams must circle all the way back to their point of view statement because something they learned during user testing made them think differently about what their user truly needs. All of these are positive outcomes for teams who have gathered feedback. The only outcome that is unacceptable is for a team to choose to ignore the feedback altogether.

Sharing Out Prototypes

After one or more iterations based on feedback, a team will begin to have a sense of the core elements of their solution and how these can be brought to life. At this point, as a design facilitator, you can urge a team to begin moving toward higher fidelity prototypes. Depending on the type of solution being proposed, there are different methods and different levels of appropriateness for bringing solutions to fruition. For example, as a student at Stanford's d.school, Molly was on a design team with a CS major and graphic designer. On this team, it was possible and useful to build a working prototype of the video feedback app that the team was developing to enhance student experiences in Massive Open Online Courses. For that class, they were also required to create a promotional video as a final presentation. Alternatively, if you are teaching in a 5th-grade classroom and students have no prior experience with coding, it would be appropriate to ask students to move from paper prototype directly to a promotional video.

When time is ample, you have one or more class periods/design sessions dedicated to the final share out. In cases like this, videos, digital presentations, and other interactive media are great forms for teams to present their process and their solution. Success of a final presentation is most likely when the goals of the presentation are clearly communicated in advance using a rubric or a checklist. When time does not permit the development of polished digital presentations, (i.e., 45–60 minutes allotted for sharing solutions), the facilitator can ask each team to say a few words about their design and then allow the entire group a few rounds of Q and A. If time is even shorter (i.e., 15–45 minutes allotted for sharing solutions), the facilitator can organize a gallery walk where one team member stays to present and other team members walk the room to observe and interact with solutions from other teams. Afterwards, roles should switch so that everyone has a chance to observe the innovation in the room.

Often, when design teams are working through a challenge, most teams are hovering in similar problem and solution spaces. The share out allows teams to identify common threads that are developed across designs as well as truly unique innovations. Given this, it is always a good practice to allot at least 15 minutes at the end of a sharing time for a facilitated whole-group discussion. Example questions include:

- In what ways were the needs identified similar across possible end-users?
- In what places were the needs drastically different from different users?
- What common elements did you observe among the solutions?
- What common themes can you identify across solutions?
- What elements did you observe that have real potential innovation in the world?

In one run of the design challenge where teachers interviewed students about their library habits (featured in Figure 4.2 above), teachers at an independent school interviewed boarding students, commuting students, international students, students with strong academics, and students who used the library as a social space. In the final share out, it became clear that every type of student was in need of a media center that could accommodate shifting needs that included quiet isolation, informal social interaction, academic group work, and digital lab time. Even though the student profiles across the times were radically different, the common need for these types of space was resounding when analyzing the sum of the prototypes.

Likewise, in a 3rd-grade project about designing dwellings for various personalities found in ancient civilizations, a group analysis of the solutions led students to propose that the common utilities of dwellings across civilizations included protection and community. These examples illustrate that when a collection of prototypes is analyzed as a whole, the value is more than the sum of its parts. The final whole-group discussion activity, when ceded with analytic questions, allows students and adult designers to elevate their critical thinking to include compare, contrast, and synthesis in a way that is much more authentic than is found in more traditional learning activities. Given this opportunity, groups can arrive at an essential understanding through comparison rather than having it delivered by teacher or textbook. In our experience, when critical information is mastered through this process, it is more likely to be retained and transferred to relevant situations than when students and adults are told what they should think is important. As such, we recommend finding the time to end prototyping and iterative cycles with some form of group sharing and intentional analytic reflection.

PART

II

Bringing Design Thinking to Life in Your Classroom

5 | Design à la carte

Figure 5.1
(Credit: Saya Iwasaki)

Molly tells this story about her introduction to design thinking:

> In the fall of 2008, I attended my first design thinking bootcamp. I went through a 1.5-day experiential challenge with Stanford's d.school and REDlab and I was hooked. I knew that this was the type of learning experience that I wanted for my students. The bootcamp started on a Friday on the streets of Palo Alto, California and concluded late Saturday on the Stanford campus. On Sunday, I went back to my classroom in East Palo Alto, prepared to integrate design thinking as a pedagogy into my lesson plans for the week.
>
> I started lesson planning the way I always do, with a list of standards I intended to cover for the week. Unlike usual, I also pulled out my design thinking handouts determined to find the intersection between these documents. I quickly felt frustrated and out of my element which was unusual for me as a teacher. I felt as if I was trying to ram a square peg into a round hole. After 2 hours of trying to make this viable, I gave up and planned lessons as usual.
>
> I later came to find that this experience was fairly common; so years later, when I began planning design thinking workshops for teachers, I was determined to mitigate the square peg round hole issue. Working with the

DOI: 10.4324/9780429273421-6

REDlab team at Stanford, we identified two ways to address this issue. The first solution is what we call design à la carte and the second was to create an alignment guide between the US national standards and the activities that are common in design thinking.

This chapter illuminates the "design à la carte" pathway for getting started with design thinking in your classroom. Chapter 1 details the alignment between design thinking and the standards.

Design Mindsets vs. Design Process

The introduction to this book outlined a set of design mindsets that are essential for teachers to cultivate as they guide the work of designers. These can be seen in Figure 5.2 and include:

- Fail forward
- Work collaboratively
- Develop creative confidence

Figure 5.2 Three critical mindsets for teachers to cultivate as they guide the work of designers
(Credit: Saya Iwasaki)

The introduction also provided a high-level overview of the design process. These include:

- Building background
- Empathizing
- Brainstorming
- Prototyping cycles

Chapters 1–4 elaborated on these four stages of the process, giving detailed examples of how these are enacted during complete design challenges.

Start-to-finish design challenges are one method for bringing design thinking into the classroom, but they are not the only method. The alternative is to bring to life the mindsets and activities associated with design thinking in one-time activities.

Design à la carte

When ordering a meal in France, you often are given a choice between a pre-fix or à la carte menu. A pre-fix menu takes you from the appetizer course through the main course and dessert, sometimes giving a diner the choice between one or two options for each phase of the meal. It is a master production by the chef. This is analogous to facilitating a complete design challenge into your classroom where you follow the process and choose one or two curated activities at each stage.

In contrast, an à la carte meal allows diners to choose food that can be ordered as separate items. Similarly, design à la carte means to free yourself of pre-set multistage process and begin the work of design thinking with standalone activities. Doing design thinking in this way allows teachers to begin building design muscles for themselves and their students. Each design-related activity is a repetition that will make the muscle stronger in preparation for a start-to-finish design challenge done at a later date. This approach increases both teacher and student confidence and competence with design thinking and is strongly recommended for beginners.

Bringing Design Mindsets to Your Classroom

As we stated in the Introduction, a mindset is an established attitude or way of thinking. Mindsets are visible through a person's words and actions. While they are often never made explicit, students perceive teacher mindsets countless times a day and often these shape how students see the world. For example, in 2009, Molly taught current events to a group of 8th-grade students and frequently watched the CNN student news. Following each news segment, she facilitated a class discussion engaging students with the topics raised in the news. Although she attempted to provide an impartial perspective, she wasn't always successful. Partway into the year, one student excitedly shared with her that when playing with his 4-year-old sister the previous day, he embodied a character from the news. He told Molly that he chased her around "roaring as a monster foreign president". This student had picked up on Molly's subtle opposition to recent international events as well as the biased introduced by CNN student news. She was shocked that her political perspective had leaked into the psyche of a student and poured out of him during imaginative play with his sister.

The story is an illustration of how the mindset of a teacher and the makers of cultural artifacts such as a student newscast can be taken up by students. Design thinking requires conscious work on productive mindsets for problem solving. We have seen how the uptake is even more profound when teachers choose to be intentional and explicit about sharing their attitudes and ways of thinking (aka mindsets).

Let's take the mindset "fail forward" as an example. There are many ways a teacher can communicate with their students about failure to change their preception that failure is to be avoided at all costs. When they stumble upon their own small "failures" in the classroom, their students are watching. For example, imagine a teacher who breaks a school rule; pulls out a phone during class, accidentally curses, or gives students some incorrect information. When they recognize this small failure, they have a couple options. They can sweep it under the rug, pretend as if it never happened, and ignore their students' insistence that it did. This shows students that they are ashamed of their mistake and that they are afraid of how it reflects on them. Alternatively, they could own the mistake and apologize profusely to the students.

Yet another option would be to be intentional, to call attention to the mistake, and to unpack it with their students. If they were trying to use this as a "fail forward" teachable moment, they might explain the circumstances leading up to the mistake and what they would do differently in the future to avoid repeating the small failure. They may ask students to share a time that they made a similar mistake and encourage them to replace any related shame with strategies for improvement. A teacher choosing this third option could further strengthen the lesson by naming their mindset explicitly "failing forward" and referring to this event in the future as the failing forward conversation. In this example, they would be bringing a mindset of design thinking to life in their classroom outside of a complete design challenge. Planned and unplanned lessons about mindsets are lessons that build design thinking muscles.

Design à la carte

When bringing design mindsets into your classroom, it is essential to prioritize those that resonate the most with you. Remember that design à la carte means selecting the item from the menu that most appeals to you. As you return again and again to design thinking exercises as a pedagogy, you can either select the same mindset or broaden your choice beyond your original selection. In either case, you are bringing one or more mindsets into the classroom culture through repeated exposure.

In the introduction, we shared the three most critical mindsets for teachers to foster. Below is an expanded list of mindsets for sharing with students. This list is also depicted in Figure 5.3. This is an orientation to these student-friendly mindsets (for the comparison to the teacher mindsets presented in the Introduction, refer to page 13). After you read each sentence below, pause and reflect on how the idea sits with your sensibility as a teacher. When you reach the end of the list, identify which resonate most deeply with you.

- **Embrace empathy:** empathy is the ability to understand the perspective of another person. Design thinkers use empathy as an entry point into problem-solving.
- **Collaborate across boundaries:** collaborating is to work together on an activity, particularly around creating something. Collaborating across boundaries means to work on diverse teams where each individual brings different skills and perspectives to the table.
- **Linger in ambiguity:** ambiguity is the quality of being open to more than one interpretation. Before posing a solution to a problem, design thinkers immerse themselves in the problem space and seek to view it from every angle.
- **Yes, and…:** yes, and… is a phrase that captures the essence of building on one another's ideas. When working together, instead of judging contributions by teammates, design thinkers listen to contributions and build on them using Yes, and….
- **Fail forward:** failure refers to a lack of success and often connotes shame and shut down. This has been historically and practically so in schools. Design thinkers reclaim failure as a positive experience and aim to fail early and often. They know that each failure illuminates necessary insights towards learning and the next success.

Bringing Design Thinking to Life

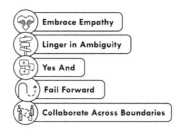

Figure 5.3 Student-friendly mindsets for teachers to share with students
(Credit: Saya Iwasaki)

Grab a pen and make yourself a note about which of these mindsets resonated most clearly with you. Place the note somewhere where you will see it often: on the bathroom mirror, on the whiteboard in your classroom, or on the dashboard of your car. When you see the note, regard it with intention. Think about an instance when you observed this mindset in your classroom or your life or think about a clear counterexample. Then, when the teachable moment arises or when you intentionally create the opportunity, bring the mindset into your classroom. Whether you teach Kindergarten, English Language Learners, or AP physics, it should not take more than a couple days before a teachable moment arises. When you see the opportunity, seize the moment. The moment might arise in the flow of classroom activities or you might plan a way to exercise it. This can be your first design à la carte activity.

Activating Parts of the Process in Your Classroom

Each stage of the design thinking process carries with it a set of common activities that can be done as part of a complete design challenge or activated as à la carte activities. Below is a list of the stages along with activities that are common at each stage.

- **Building background:** setting the space, resourcing the space, introducing real-world experts, 2 × 2 matrices, organizing students into diverse groups
- **Empathizing:** real-world observations, interviews, empathy maps, point of view statements

- **Brainstorming:** rules for brainstorming, the act of brainstorming, idea selection
- **Prototyping:** low-resolution prototypes, paper prototypes, sketching ideas, storyboarding, gathering feedback and applying it in revision

Any one of these activities can be utilized in any number of lessons or unit plans. They do not have to sit within a complete design challenge to raise the spirit of design thinking in your classroom. In fact, you may find that you do some of these things in your lessons already but whether or not this is totally new or just a new frame for existing work, utilizing design activities is another great way to do design à la carte.

Let's take empathizing as an example. If you teach language arts or humanities, one popular way to bring empathizing into your classroom is to use your text as the data for an empathy map. Remember to have the students select a character and find evidence from the text about what that character is doing, saying, thinking, and feeling. Teach students about how to make the leap from concrete data to inferences about a person's thoughts and emotional states. We have seen this done with early elementary students mapping Cinderella's experiences, upper elementary students mapping the experiences of ancient Egyptians, middle school students mapping the experiences of Boo Radley, and high school students unpacking Hamlet's experiences. Another way to bring literature and history to life through empathy is to have students become the characters and study novels or primary sources in preparation for being interviewed by their classmates. Empathy activities are versatile and can be flexibly crafted to meet the needs of any age group.

Empathy is not just for history and humanities. In science and math, empathy can provide the real-world context needed to help students understand why they are learning something. In one math class observed, the teacher used the Pokemon pokedex to identify the size of several popular pokemon. She then had students design scale model dwellings for each Pokemon, justifying how much space each would need to eat, sleep, and relax.

In another example of empathy in a science class, during a unit on water conservation, a teacher had students conduct formal observations on water usage in their school, home, and neighborhood. Rather than just using this as background building about the fact of water waste, she used it to launch a conversation about why and how water is wasted. She then

Bringing Design Thinking to Life

had students observe water practices of other cultures and compared US behaviors to international behaviors with water resources. The most profound activity among these was when the teacher had the students carry multiple gallons of water across a playground as an empathy building activity for African women who must carry water for many miles for the survival of their families.

These examples we present illustrate the types of activities that can be integrated into existing curriculum as standalone efforts to bring design thinking into the classroom. The next section introduces 12 design thinking activities that you can use immediately as a way to get started.

Design Activities to Get You Started

1. Invite students to build background on an upcoming teaching topic by requesting they bring in one artifact or article that would help others to learn something about the topic.
2. Hunt down 3 people with relevant expertise on a topic you will teach and invite them to visit or videoconference with your students.
3. Make a graphic organizer for a real-world observation (left column—what a person is doing/timestamp, right column—what a person is thinking or feeling). Ask students to observe a video relevant to what you are teaching and complete the graphic organizer.
4. Ask students their thinking about a topic you are teaching and have students gather evidence of multiple perspectives on the topic either in dialogue with one another or by searching for varying perspectives in digital sources.
5. Create an empathy map with your students that upacks the actions of a character from history, literature, or a predominant figure from your field.
6. Organize students into diverse teams and teach them explicitly about how each team member has a different set of skills and perspectives that are valuable to the group.
7. Create a 2 × 2 matrix that will support students' ability to analyze a set of elements related to what you are teaching. Ask students to work on teams to justify placement of elements on the grid

and facilitate discussion about the placement of each element. Give positive reinforcement for respectful recognition of multiple perspectives.

8. Teach the rules of brainstorming and have students brainstorm solutions to a known problem within the classroom or school.
9. Teach students a process for gathering feedback on something they have created and give them the time to collect feedback and revise their product. We like to start by asking students to first share what they like or appreciate about the creation. A later round might ask for what they "wish" relating to the creation.
10. Create wall space for groups to work on a project together and ask students to stand up within their group space for collaboration time.
11. Launch a classroom campaign to celebrate failure and allow students to point out their own moments of a failure in a way that supports their ability to grow (e.g., create a failure tree in math class and hang failed attempts as leaves on the tree).
12. Introduce the language "yes, and..." and give students positive reinforcement when the phrase is specifically used to build on one another's ideas.

These activities are effective ways for your and your students to begin building design thinking muscles. They do not carry the same level of risk as launching a complete start to finish series of activities that constitute a unit-length challenge, yet they introduce the spirit and mechanics of design thinking. Read through this list of activities one more time and select an activity that you could build into an upcoming lesson.

Teaching Design Challenges

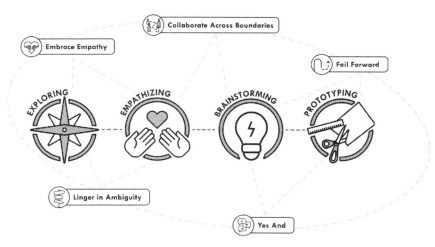

Figure 6.1
(Credit: Saya Iwasaki and Molly B. Zielezinski)

Now that you have tried some à la carte design thinking exercises, it is time to stage design thinking challenges that put the entire process and mindsets into action. In this chapter, we outline plans for design thinking challenges that will help you and your students start to understand and develop skills with the process and mindsets while having full design thinking experiences. In Chapter 5, we suggested small scenes of design thinking component activities as a way to introduce and exercise your design thinking muscles.

DOI: 10.4324/9780429273421-7

Herein, we outline three kinds of design challenges you can work with in your classroom.

The three types of challenges outlined in this chapter are the **Short**, the **Feature**, and the **Series.** Shorts are 1-hour, fast-moving, yet complete design challenges. Features are full-length, intense challenges that may take 1–3 days. They are full-scope design challenges that might also integrate specific content activities. Series are unit-length design thinking challenges. Like other units you teach, they may span a week to a month of classroom time and integrate or sit side-by-side with other standards-based content. We provide an example and outline of each. Remember that the topics of these challenges can appeal to students of a wide range of ages and skills. Still, we indicate tips for use with younger students and older students. When you add in the particulars of the skills and content you will be infusing with your design thinking activities, you will set the stage for a full design thinking challenge.

Kick-Off Design Thinking Challenges with Improv Activities

We highly recommend starting all classroom design thinking activities with a short improvisation exercise. Improv will help prepare students for the creative work they will do as part of design thinking. It will call attention to the importance of communication, help students learn to listen, and encourage full participation. Improv is often used as warm-up exercises in performance groups. Improvs are fun, and there is no real risk of failure. They are about getting in rhythm with others and setting the stage for creativity and action. Improv is an activity that prepares students to have fail forward attitudes and experiences. We often use improv activities to open challenges, and we also use them to warm up for design activities within longer challenges.

We suggest spending 2–10 minutes on improv activities. Even one quick exercise will have benefits at the start of a set of design thinking activities. We share a few that we find very effective with students and more are easy to find through web searches. Second City, an improvisation theatre in Chicago, has a page with ten reasons why teachers should use improv in their classrooms. You can find it at www.routledge.com/9780367221331. We use each of the highlighted improv activities with young students and adults. We know you will find them easy to adapt for your students no matter what grade you teach.

Counting Up and Counting Down (Young to Middle Grades Students)

Students stand in a line or circle. Students will count together from 1 to 10. Start from crouching with a whisper for #1, stand bent for and speak low for #2, rising slightly and with regular voice for #3, etc. By the time the group reaches #10, they should be loud and standing with arms above their head (and maybe jumping up). Several rounds can be conducted. Let students try to coordinate with each other as they build up the numbers. Invent variations that suit your students.

The Names of...Game: A Categorization Improv (All Ages)

Students stand in a circle. You name a category and say, "Let's go around the circle. When it is your turn, think of the name that fits that has not yet been said. This game ends when we get to a repeat. You sit or step back. We also start a new category". Examples for young students might be "Names of colors", "Names of kinds of animals", or "Names of people in our class". Older students might enjoy "Names of countries", "Names of elements in the periodic table", "Names of US elected officials", or "Names of people that start with the letter ———".

One-Word-at-a-Time Sentences (All Ages)

Students stand in a circle. You or a student starts by saying a word that can be the first word in a sentence. Each person in turn adds a new word. When anyone in the circle thinks a full sentence has been created, students put their hands together and say. "Yes, yes. Yes. yes". Then the next person in the circle starts a new sentence. Do this for a few rounds until everyone in the circle has contributed a few sentences.

Teaching Design Challenges

Sound Ball (All Ages)

In Sound Ball, students will pass an imaginary ball to each other. When they pass the "ball", they make a sound and pass it to a student they look at across the circle. The student across pretends to receive the ball and imitates the thrower's sound. Then that student makes eye contact and throws the ball to another student while making a new sound. If the first person threw the imaginary ball to you, they might make the sound "whoosh" as it was thrown. You would pretend to catch it and while saying "whoosh", then pass it as you said "zazazaza". The pattern repeats until most students have received and sent the ball once or twice. You might remind students to spread the ball around the entire circle.

Mirror Your Partner (Mid-Elementary to Older Students)

Students pair off. The objective is for students to physically mirror each other's movements. Ask students to stand in pairs and face each other. When you say "Begin", one student begins to slowly move their arms, legs, head, and face. The other student tries to mimic their partner's behaviour and expressions. After 20 seconds, ask them to reverse. The goal is for them to get in sync as much as they can each turn. You can go several rounds.

Syncing Pairs (Older Students)

Students face each other in pairs. They will take turns counting from 1 to 3. They should practice alternating the counting of 1, 2, 3 repeatedly without resetting **which of the partners starts at 1**.

In the second round, the number 1 is replaced by a hand clap. Let them practice. Remind them to slow it down as they start replacing numbers with movements.

In the next round, replace the number 2 with a foot stomp. This raises the difficulty, so notice the fun and the frustration. Stop dyads and ask students how they felt as the rules of the improv were changing. You can add a third round and replace the number 3 with a pat on the head. We also ask them why they think we do this exercise.

Rock, Paper, Scissors Sync Up (Younger and Older Students)

Students stand in a circle. When you count, 1, 2, 3, each student displays one of the three, showing rock, scissors, or paper. Usually a competition, this game's goal is to have all people in the circle display the same signal when you call for it. They are not allowed to talk to plan their moves. See if they are able to sync up after multiple rounds. For younger students, you can give them animals that they can verbally and physically imitate instead of the rock, paper, and scissors hand signals.

Rock, Paper, Scissors Competition (Older Students)

The objective of Rock, Paper, Scissors competition is for elimination rounds to result in a faceoff between two teams. We start with students in pairs where they will hold a three-round rock, paper, scissors competition. The loser joins the winner as a cheerleader for the winner team. The winner with the new team member in tow finds another recent winner. With their new teammates cheering their name, they engage another round of rock, paper, scissors with a new opponent. Again, all losers join that winner's team. In a minute there will only be two winners left in the room, each with large teams cheering them on by chanting their name. When the competition ends, hold cheers all around. Remember that under the rules rock beats scissors, scissors beat paper, and paper covers and beats rock. If players choose the same, they complete that turn over again.

Improvisation exercises mastered, it is time to start your design thinking activities.

Design Thinking Shorts

We start with introductory challenges, called a "Short". The Short is an hour-long, quick-moving, and introductory challenge that introduces designing for others, highlighting empathizing as a key process, and using a prototyping cycle. Shorts are fast-paced. While Shorts are perfect for our students and well-adapted to the classroom schedule, we find they are also wonderful for introducing parents, teachers, and other community members in your school

Teaching Design Challenges

to design thinking. A Short gives a touch of design thinking. It introduces working with a partner and raises energy and understanding of the design thinking enterprise through empathy work, brainstorming, and rapid prototyping. They usually result in creative design ideas that exceed expectations.

We do not require you to find outside design partners for Shorts, but you may do so if that is easy for you to accomplish. Shorts are structured to let students work in pairs and interview and design for each other. If your students are not yet used to working in teams, Shorts will give them an opportunity to collaborate before they have to handle group dynamics. Shorts will give them an opportunity to partner before they have to learn team collaboration. You can adapt Shorts to be team experiences, yet we caution that if you do, Shorts will take a bit longer in terms of time.

In addition to a paired collaboration, a Short provides an empathy experience and asks students to make inferences based on their empathy interviews, but initially does not introduce the Point of View (PoV) statement. Students engage in a short brainstorm and an experience with rapid prototyping. Prototyping is followed by the presentation of the prototypes to their paired design partners and soliciting feedback. Shorts conclude with sharing and reflection based on the feedback. We suggest that you use at least one Short before you try a Feature or Series design challenge.

The short activity that follows is an ungraded challenge. If you are working with younger students, you will expect more drawing and you might assist students with interviewing. For older students, you can emphasize note- and record-keeping, more elaborate prototypes, and documented revision lists. You may extend the time for this Short, but the idea is to move swiftly through the steps and keep the students' energy flowing.

Design Thinking Short Activity

How Might We Design a Home Space for Learning?

Activity Overview

This Short design thinking challenge provides students with an overview of the phases of design thinking. They work in pairs and design for each other. Students will learn that the process helps them to spark creativity and variety in their solutions.

Bringing Design Thinking to Life

Materials

- Folded paper journal for notes (two or three sheets should suffice)
- Prototyping materials
- Paper folded into eight boxes (at least one for each student)

Learning Objectives

Students will:
- Engage in a design challenge
- Synthesize information
- Brainstorm ideas
- Build a prototype
- Test a prototype and plan for revision
- Share information

Steps for the Activity

Step 1: Building Background (5–10 Minutes)

We ask students to think about their location and materials at home for school learning. We ask them to individually draw pictures of, or write down ideas for how to improve their space for schooling at home.

Once students individually produce one or more ideas, we tell them they just engaged in problem-solving. Have them share out a few ideas. Tell them we asked them to problem-solve, yet we did not require them to come up with their best ideas.

Tell them we have a process for them to solve big and small problems that will help them come up with really fun, interesting, and GOOD ideas that can make a difference to people. Tell them this process is called design thinking.

Step 2: Empathizing (15 Minutes)

Create dyads for the students. If there is one extra, make one group of three or decide to have the extra student work with you in a dyad. Tell the students that each pair will have 5 minutes to interview their partner. We advise that you give them some of the questions to answer that we propose. This will help you keep this exercise within the 1 hour range.

Questions:

- When you do schoolwork at home, where do you do it? Please describe your setup.
- Tell me what you like about this setup?
- Tell me what you do not like about this setup?
- Tell a story about a time this setup was helpful and comfortable for you?
- Tell me a story about when this setup did not work well for you.
- Have you tried other ways to set up for schoolwork at home? What were they?
- If you could imagine your best setup for school work at home, what would it be?

Put a timer on for 5 minutes and tell the students to start. At the 5-minute mark, tell them to switch who is now interviewing and who is being interviewed. If you see the students are done interviewing or not near finishing, you can shorten or lengthen the interview time intervals.

At the 10-minute mark, give each student 2 minutes to write brief notes and/or sketches on a new page of their design journal. Ask them to write one problem they would like to solve for their design partner.

You can ask for a few students to share out the problems they would like to solve if they would like but keep sharing brief in order to keep the activity moving along.

Put on upbeat music while the students draw and write ideas.
Prompt those who need help. Stop them at 8 minutes.

Step 3: Brainstorming (8 Minutes)

Brainstorming in a short is an individual activity rather than a group one. That is why we lessen the burden and ask for a less abundant list of design ideas. We suggest you use a brainstorm technique called Crazy 8s.

In Crazy 8s, you ask students to fold a piece of paper into eight boxes (three folds, each time in half). Ask them to fill each box with one idea that might solve their design partner's problem or improve their design partner's school-at-home setup. Say you expect at least one idea for each box and that they can use the back of the paper as well.

Step 4: Prototyping Cycles (20 Minutes—10 for Prototype; 10 for Sharing and Feedback with Partner)

Ask each student to choose one idea from their Crazy 8s brainstorm. Tell them they will build a prototype of the idea for their partner. Show them the materials that are available for prototyping and tell them that they are free to use these materials for their prototype. Remind them that they can build, draw, or even act out a prototype. You might allow them to use other classroom materials and resources since this is a schoolwork set up they are creating.

Remind them that they will share their prototype with their design partner, but they do not need to consult with them until sharing time. Part of the experience will be for them to allow their ideas to take charge and surprise their design partners. Remind them to think about creating something their partners can look at, touch, and question. Give them 8–10 minutes to prototype. Remind them that they will need to move quickly.

Give students a 1 minute warning on prototyping time. Then tell them they will have 5 minutes to each share prototypes and get feedback. Tell them to return to their dyad partners to share (10 minutes).

Tell the students to write notes in their design journal about the feedback they got. They should also write an idea for an improvement or change they would make to their prototype if they were moving forward.

Sharing (5 minutes)

Step 5: Closing the Activity with a Quick Process Check

Take a few minutes to close the activity by having students share. This should have a relaxed feel. There are several ways you can do this. We'd say go with what is comfortable for you. We suggest a few ways to close.

- Ask students to share a prototype that was created for them that they really appreciated.
- You can ask them if they had any surprises in the process. You might ask them which part of the process they enjoyed the most.

Teaching Design Challenges

> - At the Stanford d.school, design challenges often end with a circle and a share-out. Each person is asked to share out a thought responding to one of the following prompts:
>
>   – I like...
>   – I wish...
>   – What if...
>
> When all in the circle who wanted to speak are finished, congratulate all for finishing the design thinking challenge. Enjoy!

Feature-Length Challenges

A Feature enables the full experience of the design thinking process in an intense, fast-paced, 1 or 2-day time period. The students experience all parts of the design thinking process and encounter and develop design thinking mindsets. Features are 1 to 2-day challenges that utilize collaborative teams, design partners from outside the classroom, and result in the prototype and revision process. They can be thematic in nature, such as the challenge we share below about pet shelters, or they can take up specific topics or concepts from the curriculum.

Like Shorts, Features are energetic and intense immersive experiences. They allot time to enable deep dives into the process and mindsets and are extremely useful for teaching students design thinking. If you are an elementary teacher, taking a day or a good part of a day or two to complete a feature challenge works quite well. Shelley likes to use Features to punctuate special activity days and address topics that students are excited to work on. We have seen teachers use Features to address the setting of classroom norms, solve problems around the school such as how to better maintain safety during school end of day pick-up, how to create a student leadership group or fundraising project, or even how to plan a celebration or field trip. We have seen high school students design solutions for increasing students' campus privileges and for the design of tutoring programs. We have seen students redesign their lunchtime experiences and create Teach-Ins. Features can have much versatility in the problem spaces they address. Really, the sky's the limit.

Bringing Design Thinking to Life

It is also a good idea to integrate content coverage with design thinking Features. Upper elementary students can plan for the 100th day of school for primary students. They can create a structure for a 100th day celebration and include designs for the specific number-based activities of the younger students. If you have primary students, you might take a story and complete a character empathy activity (as we described in Chapter 2) and turn it into a Feature by adding in the PoV statement, brainstorming, and prototyping activities. High school students might create a plan for lobbying the school administration or officials out in the community about a topic of interest and concern. They might also write fan-fiction or alternative stories to meet the needs of the characters in the literature that they read.

We suggest making Feature challenges a steady part of your classroom. You and your students will learn a lot about the design thinking process and you will find topics to create challenges that have meaning for you and the students. You would develop tremendous capacity for your students if you did one Feature challenge a quarter. We highlight the pet shelter challenge discussed in Chapter 4 as a first Feature challenge you might facilitate in your classroom. We think you will enjoy exploring this challenge with your students.

Feature Challenge

Designing a Pet Adoption Experience

Activity Overview

In this challenge students will ask the question: how might we make the pet shelter adoption experience a more effective one? You can complete this challenge over the course of one day or split it over several. We do not suggest that you leave more than a day or two if you segment it. We advise against splitting a design challenge into once a week chunks of activity as it makes it difficult for students to keep up momentum. We find that students easily forget their prior progress.

Materials

- Design journal
- Markers or sticky notes, wall space or large paper on walls

Teaching Design Challenges

- Large paper or wall space for empathy and three-column charts
- PoV statement template
- Prototyping materials

Learning Objectives

1. Students will complete a design thinking cycle.
2. Students will understand the role of pet shelters and will learn about sheltering and adoption processes. Students may also learn about different pets and their requirements for shelter and care. They may learn the processes shelters use for trying to get pets adopted.
3. Students will create interview questions, interview design partners, compile, and analyze notes.
4. They will make inferences, conduct brainstorming, and learn to communicate with adults who are their design partners through soliciting feedback and planning for iteration based on it.

Standards Connection Example

Standards Next Generation Science Standards MS-ETS1. Middle School Engineering

Design MS-ETS1-1. Define the criteria and constraints of a design problem with sufficient precision to ensure a successful solution, taking into account relevant scientific principles and potential impacts on people and the natural environment that may limit possible solutions.

MS-ETS1-4. Develop a model to generate data for iterative testing and modification of a proposed object, tool, or process such that an optimal design can be achieved.

Steps in the Challenge

Step 1: Building Background (Expect 1–2 Hours and May Include Homework)

Arrange for design partners ahead of activity introduction. To set the stage for this challenge, you may want to find some family members of students or school staff and teachers who have adopted pets or might like to adopt a pet. You will want to locate three to five people who can meet with your student teams and be interviewed. We realize finding design partners can feel like a burden, but for this challenge, just find people who are willing to help out and have pets and can think about shelters and adoption processes. No expertise is necessary. They are there to share with your students and stimulate them no matter what their experience level. They could even talk to someone who is afraid of dogs or has never thought of owning a pet before. All perspectives will be interesting! Many teachers find one or two parents, a teacher or administrator in the school, or one of their friends or relatives. A local shelter you contact may be able to put you in touch with one of their volunteers or interns.

Introduce the challenge to the class. Try one of these challenge topics (or create your own based on your students and your local community resources):

- A design partner might be interested in adopting a new pet. *How might we design a home environment for the new pet?* **(Younger students to middle school)**
- A shelter would like to encourage more adoptions. *How might we design a pet adoption experience?* **(Mid-elementary to older school students)**
- A nearby animal sanctuary is planning to open a facility in town to help with their adoption processes. **(Mid-elementary to older school students)**
  - The requirements must include:
  - The space must provide shelter for three different animal species.
  - The space must support the adoption process so that as many animals as possible can find good forever homes.
  - The facility should be space and environmentally efficient and comfortable for all its residents.
- *How might we design for a new facility?* **(Older students)**

Background Research. Ask students to think about and learn about pet shelters. They will have a short amount of time. The idea is for your students to get an introduction to pet shelters and their work. You might choose one or two of the ideas we suggest.

- You might invite someone from a local shelter to speak with your students by visiting the classroom or talking with them online. You might ask to hear about the different animals they shelter and how their adoption processes work.

- You might take the class on a field trip to a local shelter so they can have a tour of the facilities. If your students are older, you might have them do research into different shelter groups, pet rescue organizations, and fostering programs.
- You might want to find information on shelters from local and national organizations and make the resources available to your students. You will want to have students complete this background research based on the skills you would like to emphasize.
- Show video or pictures of animals in a shelter or at a sanctuary.
- Maybe set a space in the classroom for their information. Tell them we have a process for them to solve big and small problems that will help them come up with really fun, interesting, and GOOD ideas. Tell them this process is called design thinking.

You will want students to share their research. If you have young students, you might have students share while you take notes on big paper. You could have older students create short presentations about their key discoveries about pets and shelters that are archived and available.

Step 2: Empathizing (2–4 Hours)

Tell the students that they are going to **design** a solution based on real situations and people's needs.

Interviewing

In Features, students gain experience creating, administering, and culling information from interviews. Some information that students may want to gain from the interviews might include:

- Some basic information about their design partners.
- Design partners experiences with pets in their lives.
- A description of their partner's current pets. How did they come to have them?
- If their design partners have ever visited a shelter, sanctuary, or other home for pets? Descriptions of the visit(s)?
- The kind of experiences they would want to have if they visited a shelter?

Bringing Design Thinking to Life

Let students each write one or two questions. Then have groups meet and compare questions and craft a final list. Also have the group members decide on group rules or review the interviewing tips in Chapter 2. One or two people would be asking questions, and one or two should be taking notes. If the students are recording, one student would monitor the recording device.

For younger students, help them interview a design partner. Let the students have 20–30 minutes for the interview. You could have the interview as a whole class activity if you have young students or if you did not find several design partners.

Gaining insights from Interviews

1. **Note-taking.** At the conclusion of the interview give students time to jot down and organize their interview notes. With younger students, help them record what they heard from the design partner. In addition to writing, you might give them time to draw a picture related to what they heard or saw. It is important to have students record what they heard, saw, and thought. Ask them to consider the following:

    - What did you find out about your partners' experiences?
    - What stood out to you?
    - What are you curious about or what surprised you?

    Let the students spend 10 minutes to jot down their interview notes. Team members may want to share during this activity.

2. **Empathy mapping.** Have them create an *empathy map* (20–30 minutes). Refer to Chapter 2 for more background on these empathy activities. Help the students realize that they will be writing descriptions of what they heard their design partner "say" and "do". They will be a bit more interpretive about what their design partner "thinks" and "feels". No doubt their design partners will tell the students how they feel or what they think. Recognize that the students are correct when they feel like they are guessing a bit about what their design partners are thinking or feeling. Remind them that they will have time to triangulate these inferences as they create a prototype and get feedback from their design partner. If they have guessed wrong about something, it will be corrected.

3. **Create a three-column chart.** Constructing a *three-column chart* will help the students build confidence and move towards empathy for their design partners. They will have the opportunity to use many adjectives to describe what they noticed about their partner. They can also clearly state needs and ideas that were expressed by the partner. Through constructing the chart and then creating links across the columns, students will start crafting contending point of view statements.
4. **Write a PoV statement.** Let each team use the template located at www.routledge.com/9780367221331. Tell the students that the next step in solving their design challenge is to write a PoV statement. They can refer to their three-column chart and choose one or two connections across the columns that they feel confident about to include them on a short list as contenders for the PoV. After discussing them, they should choose one that they would like to take on for current design purposes. Have them use the template and finish by checking their statement to make sure it meets PoV criteria.

You can ask for a few students to share out the problems they would like to solve if you would like.

Step 3: Brainstorming (8 Minutes)

As we mentioned in Chapter 3, brainstorming can take many forms. Brainstorming can be organized as an individual or group activity. We suggest that it is a good idea to let students experience both forms of brainstorming. We advised that you use Crazy 8s in Shorts. There is also a role for an individual brainstorm in Feature challenges. If you like and as time allows, you can ask your students to complete Crazy 8s as preparation for a team brainstorm. With Crazy 8s, students will come to a team brainstorm with eight ideas to bring forward. In Crazy 8s, you will ask students to fold paper into eight boxes and fill each box with one idea that might solve their design partner's problem.

With or without eight ideas, the stage should be set for students to brainstorm (see Chapter 3). Remind teams of the rules of brainstorming. Start by giving teams 5–10 minutes to come up with as many ideas as they can. Maybe suggest they aim for 25 ideas. Remind them of the guidelines:

Bringing Design Thinking to Life

- Say your idea
- Write your idea on a sticky note or in writing on a large sheet of paper
- One idea at a time
- Try to build on each other's ideas
- No evaluation of ideas. Every idea is a good one.

Circulate and encourage more and more ideas. Prompt them as necessary. Give them another 2 minutes to post another ten ideas.

Ask the students to vote on these ideas (use the method in Chapter 3 Figure 3.2 to identify the ideas they most like). Once the votes are marked, let the students choose among the ones that got votes. Sometimes groups will find a way to combine two ideas. Remember that a team may not all agree on a single idea. In that case, you might let a group prototype two ideas. Choose one of their ideas that they are most excited about and tell them this will be the idea they move forward into prototyping.

Step 4: Prototyping Cycles (20 Minutes—10 for Prototype; 10 for Sharing and Feedback with Partner)

Ask each team to choose one idea from their brainstorm. Tell them they will build a prototype of the idea for their design partner. Show them the materials for prototyping and tell them that they are free to use these materials for their prototype. Remind them that they can build, draw, or even act out a prototype. You might allow them to use other classroom materials and resources since this is a schoolwork setup they are creating.

Give students a variety of prototyping materials and tell them that they have 20 minutes to construct their prototypes. Tell the class that a prototype is not only a model but is also a way to make an experience tangible. Explain that, instead of drawing a sketch or making a scaled model, they might use furniture in the classroom. Remind them to think about creating prototypes for which their partners can interact.

Give students a 1-minute warning on prototyping time. Then tell them they will have 5 minutes to share prototypes and get feedback.

Ask the design partners to meet and give them feedback on the designs. Encourage the students to help the design partner by answering questions, but not to lecture them about the prototype. They should explore the prototype. Have a quick tour through.

Students should keep notes on the feedback they are given.

When finished, students will look over their notes, create a list of suggestions, prioritize the list into a list of revisions they would make. If there is time, let them have another 10–15 minutes to improve their prototypes.

Step 5: Sharing, Reflections, and Assessment (10–30 Minutes)

We always try to save a slot of time so projects can be shared across teams. We suggest you conduct an activity to close every Feature challenge. There are many ways you can do this. We prefer that the reflection activity is positive and upbeat. You can refer to those we outlined in the description of the Short challenge such as sharing a few prototypes or doing the "I like, I Wish, What if…" activity. Any of them can be used in a Feature challenge.

We use a variety of techniques to close projects. Some take a short amount of time and might be just right if you are coming to the end of the time scheduled for a challenge. Others can be more elaborate, such as group presentations with invited audiences. The presentations by teams take time and preparation, yet we like them because they cause groups to reflect on their processes, organize their insights, show their prototypes, and describe the feedback they have incorporated.

At the quick end of the spectrum, you could produce a gallery walk where all prototypes are on display with their PoV statements. You can give students time to walk around and see each prototype. They can then offer praise or ask questions about particular prototypes.

You can also hold a discussion, asking students to volunteer positive feedback on projects they found interesting and impressive. You can give them the prompt: "What I appreciate about this project is that…".

For a more elaborate Feature assessment, you might also want or need to have students complete an activity aimed at assessing their experience and learning. We suggest four possible assessments:

1. Build off of the process of sharing prototypes and have design partner(s) talk about how the prototypes addressed their design partner's needs. Students might find this process invigorating, especially if their partner shares positive comments classwide.
2. If design partners are not present, you can ask students to comment by asking questions about prototypes that they find

interesting. Questions such as: "What issue/problem was this prototype trying to address"? or "If you were going to do a next round, how would you change your prototype"?
3. You can hold a discussion or give students a reflection assignment that they can complete in their design journals. Ask one or more of the following questions:

   a. Can you describe your favorite part of this challenge?
   b. What changes did your team include in the prototype/concept based on feedback? What about your solution worked? What needed improvement?
   c. What did you learn from talking with your design partner?
   d. What went well for your design team? What could be improved?
   e. What did you learn about pet shelters and/or the adoption process?

4. If you have teams present their work and can provide them with time (30–75 minutes) to organize their final presentations, this can be a wonderful celebration and productive end of Feature projects. While you do not want to depress the energy of the challenge at its end, you may want to use a rubric to help assess the students' challenge activities and also help them better understand what to include in a presentation and sharing of their project work and their solutions. The presentation itself is an activity that enables student learning.

Here are some rubric items we suggest. These can be used by the students as self-assessments or completed by design partners, you, or visitors who can give feedback to the design groups on their presentations. Our advice is to keep it simple.

Ask students to comment on each team's design presentation on the following points: make sure to add any item that would make the rubric items compatible with your particular emphasis for the project. You could create a rubric with a three-point scale such as from **Not Mentioned** to **Well-described** to **Received Special Attention**. You can indicate the levels of performance using any set of terms that fit the norms of your classrooms.

1. **Teamwork:** the team explains/shows the ways they worked together, shows an example of teamwork in action.
2. **Background research:** the team could describe the background information they reviewed or consulted.
3. **Empathy/user-centered approach:**
   i. You understand how students interacted with their design partner and was insightful about them.
   ii. There is evidence that the design was inspired by the design partner.
4. **Capture needs:** the group had a clear PoV statement that included a description of the design partner and their needs.
5. **Brainstorm:** there was evidence of extensive brainstorming of possible solutions.
6. **Prototype and feedback:** the group explained their process, the prototype, and how they incorporated feedback from a design partner.
7. **Reflections on design thinking:** the team was reflective about their experience with design thinking.
8. **What was learned about shelters:** the group indicates they understand their purposes, how they work, and what needs they have.
9. **Presentation features:** the presentation highlights aspects of the challenge and the design that were significant to the team's process and design solution. Some topics that the team members might assess are: their teamwork and collaboration; their orientation to their design partners; their brainstorming effectiveness; their ability to listen to feedback and use it to improve their design.

The Design Thinking Series

A Series is a unit-length design thinking challenge that is also integrated with standards-based content. The design challenges might run for two to four weeks of classroom time, being taught in 30–60 minute time intervals. Series can be single-subject or multi-subject focused. We have seen teachers use series length design challenges in quite effective ways. We have seen these challenges taught in elementary and middle school classrooms, high schools, and in summer schools and camps. We introduce one Series

Bringing Design Thinking to Life

challenge, *The Antarctica Project*, and provide links to others that we have developed.

Facilitating a unit like the Antarctica Project is a formidable challenge. We suggest this project because we have worked out the integrating pieces and can provide you with links to the materials and resources you will need. If teaching a unit that is integrated with math is not your thing, take a look at other units we have produced that integrate content learning with design thinking. You can find them at the d.loft website (https://dloft.stanford.edu/resources). There are three full units there that take up some of the world's most pressing problems: access to and conservation of water, energy, and shelter. These topics are cross-subject in nature and fit well with design thinking tasks. **Remember that you can also create your own challenges** depending on the content you are teaching and how you can imagine an applied set of problems that it might help address.

We outline the Antarctica Project and give you tips for teaching it. We mentioned this project in the section called "How to Build Background" in Chapter 1. We have developed this math and design thinking unit over many years and have used it with many teachers and students. We are delighted to finally make it available. The project is a favorite for us because it integrates design thinking with mathematics content on functions, scale, proportion, measurement, and optimization. The project was originally developed for middle school, but we have seen it successfully used in upper level elementary classrooms and high school classrooms. Herein, we describe the project, give advice about how to best organize it, and lay out the movement between the design thinking process and math content learning. We provide a link to the written unit with all of the unit materials and activities.

Feature Challenge

The Antarctica Project

Activity Overview

In the Antarctica Project, students use functions to solve a complex, real-world problem—the design of an Antarctic research station that will house four research scientists. The unit also includes math activities that involve functions, measurement, scale, area, perimeter, and surface area concepts, as well as some computation practice.

The students role-play architects designing the new research station to meet the needs of the scientists who will winter-over in it as they complete their research. The project has engineering aspects as the students design based on empathy and a requirements list that includes personal and group living quarters, scientific workspaces, while minimizing the cost to build and heat the station.

Each phase of the project introduces new design challenges, requirements for revising prototypes, and integrated math challenges. Students have the opportunity to learn and practice new concepts about functions and apply other maths. Every concept is used to help the design meet the scientists' needs and use maths to properly represent and make a case for their design.

The question of this challenge is: how might we design a research station for a group of scientists who will winter-over in Antarctica while meeting the requirements? This project will take from two weeks to four weeks of classroom time depending on how much math you want to cover and how many design cycles you allow.

Materials

- The Antarctica Project curriculum will be available at www.routledge.com/9780367221331
- Scientist biographies will be available at www.routledge.com/9780367221331
- Design journals of 10–20 pages
- Markers, sticky notes, wall space, or large paper on walls
- Large paper or wall space for empathy and three-column charts
- PoV statement template
- Prototyping materials
- Overhead transparencies

Learning Objectives

Students will:

- Complete one or more cycles of the design thinking process.
- Create interview questions, interview design partners, compile, and analyze notes.
- Make inferences, conduct brainstorming, and learn to communicate their ideas through soliciting feedback and planning for iteration based on it.

Bringing Design Thinking to Life

Mathematics Content

Example topics by grades from the **Common Core Standards Mathematics Standards (2010):**

Grade 5

- Apply and extend previous understandings of multiplication and division.
- Convert like measurement units within a given measurement system.

Grade 6

- Understand ratio concepts and use ratio reasoning to solve problems.
- Solve real-world and mathematical problems involving area, surface area, and volume.

Grade 7

- Draw, construct, and describe geometrical figures and describe the relationships between them.
- Solve real-life and mathematical problems involving angle measure, area, surface area, and volume.

Grade 8

- Define, evaluate, and compare functions.
- Use functions to model relationships between quantities.

Some Tips on Teaching With This Feature Length Challenge

We describe the challenge by design thinking cycles and related activity. Materials in the linked curriculum documents are included for each activity including, the instructions, assessments, handouts, and answer sheets you need for that activity.

Memos: students play the role of architects in a design firm who use design thinking. Each math topic and new aspect of the design challenge is

Teaching Design Challenges

introduced in a memo from the chief designer. In this unit your students will experience multiple cycles of the design thinking process and prototyping.

Modular activity structure: the unit was constructed with a modular design. You can:

- Stop at any point and the activities completed will feel valuable and complete.
- Add your own activities, extensions, and challenges to meet your curriculum standards.
- Eliminate any activities that are not appropriate for your students. Once students create their initial scale drawing design, most of the other tasks do not depend on the activities previous to them.

Differentiation support: the unit is constructed so it can offer practice skills and extensions for advanced work, allowing for differentiation.

Collaboration plus individual work: developing the mindsets around collaboration and teamwork are developed and highlighted in these challenges. Still, the unit is designed so you can assess math learning individually.

Grading: the unit includes two quizzes, a final report, and a unit test. Students also earn points for assignments. You can assign a unit grade based on the percentage of the total points students earn during the unit.

Steps in the Challenge

Step 1: Building Background (Expect 1–3 Hours and May Include Homework)

The Antarctica Project begins with setting the stage for understanding scientific missions in the special environment that is Antarctica. One of the reasons we love to situate this design thinking challenge in Antarctica is because the continent is so unusual. It is equally unknown and strange to most students, yet is a center of international collaborations in science research. The idea of wintering-over in the isolated and hostile Antarctica environment puts scientists living under extreme conditions, yet scientists do so because they can learn so much about our planet and others in the universe. Through setting the stage, students can learn about Antarctica's geography and importance.

Bringing Design Thinking to Life

Finding materials to set the stage for learning about Antarctica is a good first step to take. Your school librarian or media specialist may be able to help you find ready resources. NASA and the NSF both have active Antarctica webpages. You might want to put some books about Antarctica in your classroom. There are also many video resources available.

We integrate some math activities in the stage setting work. We suggest you have your students complete these activities when you first introduce them to the unit as part of the background building stage. Once the students see the challenge, they will know that the initial activities are preparing them for the floor plan design work they will initially be doing. In these initial activities, students will be:

- Receiving and reviewing Memo 1 (see Figure 6.2). It will introduce the task.
- Conducting research about Antarctica.
- Preparing to work with proportionally scaled icons in their floor plans.
- Gaining comfort with conversions to metric measurements.

As you can see, background building involves both preparation for the design work and the math involved. You will want to establish teams for the project so students can collect, interpret, and share their work to build background for this challenge.

Once students see the Antarctica memo, they will be ready to start building background. You might take the equivalent of a classroom period to do a short introductory activity (e.g., show a media segment on Antarctica) and let them research and cull information and images for their notes. They may want to bookmark notable sites of information. The unit provides information on Antarctica, but we always found students enjoyed finding and exploring further resources.

There are three math activities related to background building. Choose one or all that might be useful to your students. They can make a tape for metric measurement, figure out some metric conversations (since all measurement here meets the international use of Standard measurements) and prepare to use the scaled architectural icons and the 1-cm dotted/grid paper for populating their floor plans.

Teaching Design Challenges

MEMO ONE

To: ANTARCHITECTS

From: Booker Vega, Principal Designer

Re: Welcome new hires!

Greetings and welcome to **ANTARCHITECTS**, a design and architecture firm specializing in designs for cold climates. We aim to meet the needs of our clients. We hope you'll feel right "AAT" home in your new job. We also hope you're ready to get right to work because we've got a hot (or rather, cold) new client: **The Frozen Scientific Group.**

Frozen Scientific needs to build a new research station in Antarctica, where their scientists study climate change. They had to abandon their current research station because of flooding near the site. They have decided to relocate to a nearby site further from the coast.

You will be designing the main building of the station for the four scientists who live there year-round. They expect to use the station for 20 years. Here are the requirements.

1. The site is a field of flat dry rock, 15 meters x 20 meters.
2. The building includes:
    - Sleeping quarters for four scientists
    - 1 bathroom
    - Research lab (need at least 36 square meters of floor space for equipment)
    - Entryway for storing, putting on, and taking off outdoor clothing.
3. Livability: You must make the design meet the needs of the scientists who will be there for over one year.

Frozen Scientific will judge the designs according to two criteria:
1. Includes all required rooms and fits on site (30 points).
2. Layout of is clever and attractive, uses space efficiently, and is responsive to the lifestyle and needs of the researchers in a harsh climate. (30 points).

Figure 6.2 Memo 1—introduction to the Antarctica design challenge (The Antarctica Project is a middle-school multi-disciplinary mathematics unit written by the Middle-school Mathematics through Applications Project (MMAP).)

Step 2: Empathizing (2–4 Hours)

In this challenge we use a written, character-based empathy process. The written descriptions give your students access to the kinds of persons that

145

are willing to research in extreme conditions while eliminating the need to speak with them personally.

We include links to profiles for 12 Antarctic scientists. You can see an example of a profile in Figure 6.3. The profiles enable the students to engage

Karla Petrone
Physicist

Who I am and what I do
I always knew I wanted to be a scientist. As a kid I first became interested in outer space. But when I first saw pictures of the Aurora borealis, I realized that there are many interesting phenomena that take place in the closer space that surrounds the Earth. I studied to become a physicist so that I could understand the atmosphere.

What will I study in Antarctica?
I will study the Aurora Australis or Southern polar lights, which can best be observed from Antarctica. These are natural lights of different colors that can be seen in the sky, and which are caused by solar winds flowing past the Earth. Changes in the atmosphere affect polar lights. I want to understand how this relates to climate change.

How do I like to work?
To best study the atmosphere, I often have to work when the sky is dark. I go to bed early and wake up in the middle of the night. I spend several hours looking through a telescope. It's important for me to have a good selection of audiobooks and music to listen to at those quiet times. Also, I have a voice recorder that I use to take notes as I'm observing the sky. I later have to transcribe them to my notebook, which is not my favorite thing.

What I like most about my job
Apart from science, I have always loved photography and art, so I'm fortunate I get to work outdoors in far away places and study the beautiful polar lights. I have an amazing collection of pictures of the sky, which I can share with my friends and with other photographers interested in Nature.

Also, being a physicist, I know quite a bit about electronic circuits. In the past I have been able to use this knowledge to repair and adapt equipment belonging to other scientists. However, since I'm awake mostly at night, some times they can't seem to get hold of me when they need me.

How do I like to live?
I like to keep in touch with my friends from all over the world, and to share the pictures I take with them. I also like to cook, invent new recipes and have people try them. I wonder if I'll be able to do it in Antarctica. Practicing yoga is an important part of my daily routine.

Figure 6.3 Sample Antarctica bio

(The Antarctica Project is a middle-school multi-disciplinary mathematics unit written by the Middle-school Mathematics through Applications Project (MMAP).)

Teaching Design Challenges

in an empathy process. Since the research station will house four scientists who will work and live in it, each student in a group should have a scientist for whom they design. The group will have the task of creating common spaces and scientific workspace that works for the group of scientists. That gives every student the chance to complete empathy work for one scientist, while also imagining the kinds of group living spaces that might be needed.

The link to all 12 scientist profiles can be found at www.routledge.com/9780367221331.

Empathy Activities:

1. Based on reading their scientist profiles and what they have learned about Antarctica, have students imagine and write a schedule for a typical workday for their scientist. They might include an actual schedule.
2. Have each generate a needs list for their scientist. "What does your scientist need for work and for personal space"? We suggest the following activities to have students exercise their empathy muscles:
   - Have the groups complete a three-column chart for each of the scientists. This will have them describing and stating their needs as well as a rationale for the needs they choose to bring forward into the design.
   - They might also prioritize the most important needs of each scientist in a PoV statement to see if some needs should be included in design considerations even though they might only be necessary for one scientist. They should produce a final needs list.
   - The students should look for convergence on needs across their scientists.

Step 3: Brainstorming (10–45 Minutes)

Students can bring their needs list and their PoV statements together for the brainstorm. They can put up ideas they have for their scientists individually and also then brainstorm as a team, as they make suggestions for the common spaces. We have seen big and creative ideas come from these brainstorms.

Go over good and bad brainstorming rules. Let the students spend some time voting for and prioritizing the ideas that are generated. They will want to make sure their scientist is thriving, so maybe let each student place a star next to four ideas that will be particularly important for their scientist.

Let them get creative. We have seen hot tubs, spas, media spaces, and even bowling alleys in student designs. We have also seen private spaces with insulation for music making and special spaces for scientific equipment.

Step 4: Prototyping Cycles in 2D and 3D

In this first prototype, we have students sketch a possible design on dotted/grid paper. We ask them to tape a piece of overhead transparency over their grid paper and use a nonpermanent marker so they can erase and redo as they sketch. They will be drawing this sketch to scale. They can use the architectural icons they cut out to help them judge the scale and proportion. They should also mark lengths in the scaled and real-world lengths on walls.

Have the students take the time to review each other's sketches. Start this activity with a positive team improv to remind them they have good energy to make things happen as a group. This is an opportunity for more brainstorming and discussion. Prompt them with positive ways to give feedback. Ask them to point out the features of each other's design that they really appreciated and would like to see included as they step forward. Have them ask each other if they included an item that meets their scientist's high-priority needs.

In their design journals: ask them to make sure that every scientist has needs that are being met. If not yet, have them put those needs on a list for next designs. Ask students to evaluate whether rooms seem to be reasonably sized.

Have the class participate in a class-wide design review. This will enable other students to ask questions of the first drafts and to make sure they are meeting the inferred needs of the scientists. The design review also allows you to see if students are working to scale and metric measurement in their designs.

Teaching Design Challenges

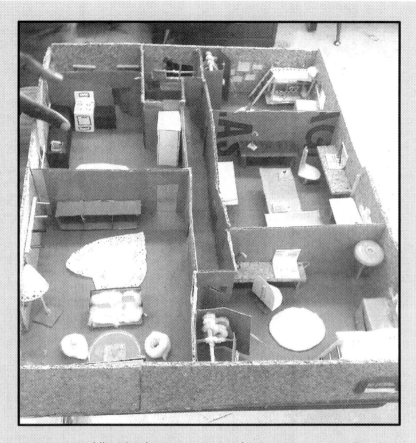

Figure 6.4 Middle school team prototype of Antarctic science station (Credit: Molly B. Zielezinski)

Step 5: Prototyping Cycles with Increasing Revisions and Requested Modifications

Follow the first round of prototype design activities with a review of area and perimeter. The activity can help them see that they can reduce their station costs without losing floor area by making it more square. They write their first **function**—to calculate the total cost of exterior walls for their design and distinguish variables and constants. This activity is coordinated by a Memo 2 from their firm's principal designer asking them to reduce the costs of their station design.

Once they work out changes, the students will receive their next Memo, 3 that asks them to now reduce surface area to make their design more efficient. They will be asked to conceive a two-story design to solve this problem. As you can see, the prototyping and feedback cycles are coming quickly and each is bringing in new math skills and opportunities to put them to use.

The prototyping cycles will ask students to create a 3D model of their Antarctica station design and to optimize heating and insulation costs. Again, you should balance moving ahead and including these activities with the time you have to spend. You can see an example of a 3D model generated by Molly's middle school grade students in Figure 6.4. Each will give students a new way to think about their design, keep scientists needs out front, and work on their math skills. You should plan to incorporate the prototyping cycles that will be of most value to your students.

Step 6: Reflection and Assessments

The Antarctica Project is a content-integrated design thinking unit. Thus, you will be wanting to assess both design thinking and math skills. In Memo 5 of the curriculum, students are asked to submit their final design and analysis of them to their design firm. The questions they are asked result in having them produce documentation of the math and design work they have accomplished. They are also asked to complete a new design task—the development of an additional small structure for the site that has just received approval. This task mimics their original units tasks and produces information that will help you assess their levels of understanding.

In addition to the final assessments, you might want to convene one more design circle to let students share and listen to the quick impressions this kind of learning experience has instilled. You might ask them to each state a word or a phrase that describes their experience of this unusual type of learning experience. Move around the circle, or just call on students when they indicate that they are ready. We sometimes pass a "talking stick" for this kind of activity.

Again, let them know how you feel about the different kinds of activity you saw them engaged in during the unit. Even a short review will send them away feeling that they are confident and efficacious learners.

Linked Materials

The Antarctica Project full unit materials. (https://drive.google.com/file/d/13fpFl0Iusrz1RJD1wnXFB75BvGWIt_HK/view)

Antarctica Scientist Profiles (https://drive.google.com/file/d/13fpFl0Iusrz1RJD1wnXFB75BvGWIt_HK/view)

Reference

National Governors Association Center for Best Practices. (2010). Common Core State Standards (Mathematics) National Governors Association Center for Best Practices, Council of Chief State School Officers, Washington D.C.

Bringing It All Together

Design thinking is within reach, and through the activities we've outlined, it can be adopted for your students' needs. We hope you have been inspired by some of the shared stories about how we and others have implemented design thinking, In addition, we hope you are able to make use of the lesson plans and activities we have suggested. One point to remember is that, in all the stories we related, the teachers and students we worked with were exploring design thinking as beginners and novices. We have not suggested anything in this book that requires you to be an expert.

Our biggest point of advice is to suggest that you do what works for you. You can use the charts in Chapter 1 to assess where you have already developed skills that are complementary or overlap with design thinking.

We've described the design thinking process and the ideas and mindsets behind it. We've also suggested ways to start bringing design thinking into the classroom. When Molly first participated in a design thinking challenge, she was part of a group of teachers from her school. She immediately started to use design shorts with her students. Once she was confident and felt ready, she had the class working on the month-long Antarctica challenge. That is one way to start. Another is to dip into a few of the à la carte activities outlined in Chapter 5.

You may want to start with a few of the activities that can help you start the design thinking engines and exercise your muscles. We have worked with many teachers over the years who started this way. The à la carte option allows you to start with the activities that seem most relevant to your specific circumstances and the needs of your classroom. After you attempt some à la carte activities, try some shorts. We say to start small, developing

DOI: 10.4324/9780429273421-8

design and mindset practices with your students. We urge you to just go for it without over-planning. It can be a small risk and a good learning opportunity for both you and your students.

That brings us to our second point. TRY design thinking activities and learn from what you do. As you know, we believe in a fail forward mindset. That means you can try activities, but don't expect them to be perfect in the first round. When you try a design thinking activity, reflect on what worked and what did not. You might keep a design journal of your own or a file. Write down or make a mental note about how you might change it the next time you will use it. Think of your classroom as a lab and train yourself into a fail forward attitude. Here's how it went for Shelley.

> The first time Shelley did a brainstorming activity with 6th graders, she let them sit at their table groups. It was difficult to get the students to make contributions and post their ideas to the poster paper that was on the table. They were not sure who could write or what to say. The energy for a productive brainstorm was just not there. They came up with ideas, but they did not generate many or build on each other's. The students did not seem energetic.
>
> The next time Shelley tried brainstorming with the students, she made the students stand up and move away from their tables. She even moved the tables vertically so the students would stand. She stacked the chairs in the corner of the room. And instead of giving everyone a marker to write ideas, she shifted to giving each student a packet of sticky notes with their markers, so they could generate notes and place them on the shared board. She also played energetic music. The changes resulted in a 180 degree turnaround. Shelley went from thinking brainstorming was difficult with children to thinking it was energetic and fun. It was easy to learn from that first failure. We tell this story to remind you to make sure to embrace a fail forward attitude in this work. Even with years of experience, we still reflect and improve every time we try an activity.

Failing forward is not the only mindset that will become important, but it may be the one that is most difficult to learn and embody. In education we stress how bad failure is, and as teachers we are also used to the pressure of making our plans work the first time we try them. We suggest you apply the fail forward mindset the same way you apply other teaching practices that you use regularly. For example, if you facilitate reading groups, you might have a basic set of practices and routines you use, but you are probably used to changing them up to keep kids involved or work with them on specific skills or objectives. Treat design thinking activities you bring to your classroom in a similar way. The design thinking process is stable as a general method and you can innovate on it to meet your students' needs. A fail forward mindset encourages you to build confidence and learn to master facilitation of design thinking skills as you go. We always encounter issues, we always change it up, and we always are up for trying something new. We never stop learning how to be better design thinkers as we are always striving to be better teachers.

As you start to engage in the process, you will see that the elements of the design thinking process and the mindsets are useful in other aspects of your teaching and in your students' learning. The skills, learning, and capabilities students will gain from the design thinking process such as writing and conducting interviews, partnering with people of all ages and walks of life, brainstorming, building models and representations, and presenting and reflecting on their ideas are all critical skills for life in the 21st century. We also know that the development of learning-related mindsets is critical for students. Remember to feel confident that your students will be learning valuable skills and dispositions through engaging in the process. Combining that with the standards-based content learning helps bring learning environments that you can feel confident and proud of as you start engaging design thinking in your classroom.

You will find that you and your students are on a journey of discovery. You might be an early adopter who likes to try new teaching practices and technologies. If you are, design thinking will give you plenty to discover (but without overwhelming you). If you work in a school where teachers are encouraged to explore and do project work, you might like to find a collaborator with whom to plan, share, and reflect. Collaborating is a key mindset in design thinking, so we encourage you to do so when and if you can. Some teachers we know make connections by concentrating design challenges on school improvements. If you do, you can involve the teachers, student, parents, and staff members as design partners. They will not fail to be impressed by the students' ingenuity. They will become allies in your work.

We close with one more point of advice. Step back and watch. Feel gratitude and joy when you see the spark in your students' eyes and their satisfaction upon learning. Shelley's group was field testing a series-length design challenge on water access and conservation (now available on the d.loft website https://dloft.stanford.edu/resources). Shelley was visiting the

Bringing It All Together

Figure 7.1 Working prototype to hydrate the dog while conserving water
(Credit: Shelley Goldman)

classroom during the prototyping phase. One boy said he was designing a device that would deliver a small stream of water from a half-gallon container into a bowl for his design partner's dog on summer days. The design partner had been worried about leaving a hose on all day while the family was gone because it would waste water. The boy was proud as he showed his prototype (see Figure 7.1). Shelley saw that the device was a siphon through a small tube, which was determining the amount of flow. She asked him if he ever heard of a siphon. He was delighted as he mentioned how he remembered that his family members had used a siphon to put gas in an empty tank. He was so pleased at his invention and doubly pleased that he actually imagined and built a working version of a widely used device. He asked, "Is this engineering"? When Shelley said, "absolutely", he smiled ear-to-ear and beamed. He said if that's what it was, he'd like to do it more, then turned to his friends, and repeated that it was engineering to his classmates.

This is the kind of experience we know every student can have when they feel responsive and efficacious in their school work. We want every student to have this kind of discovery process while they are in school.

These experiences are the ones students will remember and the kinds that can open them up to new ideas, identities, and vistas. It's why we think design thinking is transformational learning, and it's why we advocate for it. We want you to see your students have these experiences when you embark on design thinking with them. We urge you to step back when they are engaged in activities, ask them what they are doing, and enjoy their explanations of their ideas and inventions. Or just step back in a moment when the students are all heads down working together and the room has that buzz of energy. Enjoy that this is the feel of engaged learning. One teacher we know told us that she has been teaching for 20 years and doing design work in the classroom was the first time she had experienced the kind of classroom she had always imagined. The joy your students will experience and the sense of purpose will be very compelling. And to top it off, they will be engaged and learning new skills, content, and mindsets.

Printed in the United States
by Baker & Taylor Publisher Services